OAKWOOD PRESS

# BULLEID'S SR
# STEAM PASSENGER
# STOCK

## DAVID GOULD

# THE OAKWOOD PRESS

© Oakwood Press 1994

ISBN 0 85361 467 9

Typeset by Oakwood Graphics

First Edition 1980
Second Edition 1994

Printed by Alpha Print (Oxford) Ltd, Witney, Oxon.

*Other Oakwood Press books by the same author:*
  Bogie Carriages of the South Eastern and Chatham Railway
  Maunsell's Steam Carriage Stock
  SE&CR in the 1914-18 War
  Southern Railway Passenger Vans

Published by
The OAKWOOD PRESS
P.O. Box 122, Headington, Oxford.

# Introduction

Robert Holland Martin, Chairman of the Southern Railway Company, was anxious that the appearance of the steam carriage stock should be improved. Although the coaches of Richard Maunsell, the Southern's Chief Mechanical Engineer, were sound and of solid construction, they were beginning to look a little old-fashioned by 1937; moreover, a complaint had been made in 1935 that the sage-green livery was too dowdy. Shortly before Sir Herbert Walker, the General Manager, retired in October 1937, he had decided (so the story goes) what the new livery should be by reference to a length of spectacle cord; this was the colour later to be known as 'Bulleid Green' or 'Malachite Green'.

Maunsell also had announced his retirement in 1937. A new Chief Mechanical Engineer would be needed, and Walker wanted one with a dynamic personality who would carry out the necessary improvements. After soundings, he decided that Oliver Vaughan Snell Bulleid of the London & North Eastern Railway would be just the man; and so, in May 1937, invited him to make formal application for the post of CME. This was accepted, and Bulleid took up his duties on 31 October 1937, the day that Maunsell retired.

O.V.S. Bulleid was interested in carriages as well as locomotives and, although no new steam stock was designed and built immediately, much restyling was carried out on certain Maunsell coaches, particularly for the prestigious 'Bournemouth Limited' train. Features which had been introduced by him on the LNER now appeared on the Southern. Compartments were transformed with paint (pale yellow or stone) in place of the traditional stain and varnish; new oriental-style upholstery, pale green or pale pink; and incandescent tube-lighting. Oval mirrors replaced maps in the compartments, and corridors were panelled in blue rexine (a synthetic leathercloth). Externally, the coaches were painted in the new light green.

Bulleid was also very keen on welding as a method of saving weight, and the cabs of the '2-HAL' electric units of 1939 were entirely of welded construction. By the end of 1939, drawings and techniques existed for constructing the whole of a bodyside on a jig. There was only one jig for each body shell layout, so it was not possible to construct all the coaches intended for a set train simultaneously. All brake coaches were constructed the same way round, and so when the time came for sets to be formed, one of the brakes would have to be turned, using the triangle behind the locomotive works at Eastleigh. In the 1949-51 period, normally three coach bodies would be under construction at any one time: suburban motor coach, suburban trailer, and one class of steam-hauled coach. Coach underframes, which were made at Lancing, were often stored for lengthy periods, and so were complete coaches.

Bulleid coaches were built in four distinct styles. The first was the side-

3

door type, on both 58 ft and 63 ft 5 in. underframes; layout was similar to that of Maunsell stock. Next came a series with large windows and small ventilators (1947/8); then the contractor-built series with rather shallow windows and detail differences from the Eastleigh-built vehicles; and finally the series with large window ventilators, all built to SR designs but after the dissolution of the Company. The 1938 interior decor had gone out of favour, and interiors were all stain-and-varnish.

Each individual type is described in the following sections; but it would be as well to note some of the common features first. Dimensions of Bulleid carriages were completely standardised after the initial short sets. Overall length (buffers extended) was 67 ft 1 in., body length 64 ft 6 in., bodyside length 63 ft 6 in., and length of underframe 63 ft 5 in. Body width 9 ft. Height from rail to roof centre, 12 ft 4 1/2 in. Height from roof centre to top of periscope, 8 3/8 in. Bogie wheelbase, 8 ft. Bogie centres, 46ft 6in.

Bogies were SR standard. Bulleid did not think it worthwhile to introduce a new design because, even though the riding qualities were not exemplary, the bogies were easy to make and maintain.

It was not thought worthwhile to go over to all-steel construction for coach bodies, either, because of the expense of setting up enormous jigs for the relatively small number of corridor coaches being built, in contrast to contemporary electric suburban stock, which was all-steel, with small windows and could thus be fabricated in small jigs. So corridor stock was constructed with steel and timber body-framing, steel-sheeted, and wooden roofs covered with canvas. No gutters were fitted, and so rain water would pour down the bodyside, find its way into every little crack and crevice, and ultimately be the cause of extensive rusting. The steel panels would sometimes work loose and the butt-welded joints would split; these would be repaired and kept in place by steel strips.

Windows, which had glass curved to the contour of the bodyside, were mounted in steel frames which were bolted to brackets welded to the inner face of the body panel. The glass was held in place by a rubber strip compressed between two pressed steel frames. Coaches built by Birmingham Railway Carriage & Wagon Co. had window frames of Alpax alloy.

First-class compartments had medium-walnut wood veneers, grained and varnished, while the veneers in third-class compartments were light mahogany, grained and varnished. Upholstery in the 'firsts' was either deep green moquette or a deep bluish shade, with pattern. Third-class upholstery was a patterned moquette of deep brown-red in the first series of coaches and a brighter red in later examples. Metal fittings were chromed, and corridor handrails were also metal in place of the wooden rails to be found in Maunsell coaches.

Bulleid's coaches were an expression of the Southern Railway's desire to

give its customers as much comfort and spaciousness as it could afford. In this the Company was successful, and the coaches were deservedly popular. The design was so good that the BR Standard stock that began production in 1951 was largely 'cribbed' from it; overall dimensions were exactly the same, the curved bodyside was similar, and even the layout of such types as the corridor third, open third, and corridor composite was almost identical. The only improvement was in their being of all-steel construction, with steel roofs. Long after standard stock had been introduced on fast trains on the other Regions, Bulleid stock was still in regular use on the 'crack' Bournemouth and West of England train services.

In compiling this fairly detailed survey, I have been greatly assisted by Mr. Michael King, who, through his various 'contacts', has supplied building and withdrawal dates taken from official registers in private hands (there is still no post-War carriage register at the Public Record Office, Kew). Mr. Denis Cullum, who has long studied SR rolling stock, kindly loaned several Carriage Working Notices, from which the 'All round' workings shown within these pages were compiled. Mr. Laurence Mack, of the former Southern Carriage & Wagon Society, has considerable knowledge of SR stock, much of it gained from personal observation, and sent me several notes, including some on the mysterious saloon No. 100 S, and the location of condemned stock in sidings. Mr. Richard Casserley contributed Order Numbers and withdrawal dates which he had copied some years ago from official record cards. Grateful thanks to all four gentlemen.

Published sources of information on Bulleid coaches include *The Model Railway Constructor*, which published a very fine series of drawings by 'VE' between January and November 1967, some of which had previously appeared in 1951, 1952 and 1954; *Bluebell News* (good descriptions of carriage restoration); *Southern Railway Magazine* Vol. 23 p. 167, Vol. 25 p. 2 and 198; and *Railway Magazine* Vol. 92 p. 31, Vol. 93 p. 53 and 355, Vol. 95 p. 282, 300, 416, Vol. 96, p. 570. *Bulleid of the Southern*, by H.A.V. Bulleid (Allan, 1977) includes some references to coaching stock.

Finally, some of the remarks made in the following pages have been based partly on study of dated photographs, and partly on personal observation.

## THE 1945/6 3-COACH CORRIDOR SETS

Although the coaches forming these sets had an internal layout very similar to that of the pre-1936 steam corridor stock - complete with side doors leading into every compartment - the construction techniques were quite different. Maunsell's coaches had been timber-framed with body panels of steel; Bulleid's new carriages comprised steel ribs welded to a continuous flange plate which was welded on to the underframe, steel body panels welded to the main ribs and bolted to intermediate wooden ribs, and a steel cantrail. Roofs, however, were wood, covered with canvas. Underframes were similar to those of Maunsell coaches, and the standard SR 8 ft steam bogie was perpetuated.

The coaches were ordered for construction in 1940 - but only the underframes were completed. The materials for bodywork were ordered and delivered; these were then stowed away in sidings, grounded coach bodies and vans or sheds until such time as construction could start. Some of the new coach underframes, constructed at Lancing to Lot No. 7796, were appropriated in 1943 as open wagons to run between Eastleigh and Brighton Locomotive Works and numbered 1791S to 1794S in the service vehicles list. By December 1945 they were no longer required for this purpose, and it is believed that they were then employed as underframes for the new sets which by that time were under construction.

In the autumn of 1944, the Eastleigh works foreman received a memorandum instructing him to 'gather together materials and construct 22 three-coach corridor sets'. The materials were available, and so construction went ahead without delay.

The first sets, numbered 963 to 980 (Order No. 3043), comprised two five-compartment Third Brakes and a Composite with four first - and three third - class compartments. Body length was 59 ft on 58 ft underframes - the same as Maunsell steam stock. The bodyside profile was a continuous curve, using continuous steel sheet from solebar to cantrail; in later years this showed a tendency to come adrift from the body framing, and required several vertical beading strips to keep it in position. Bulleid standard doors were used; they were pressed steel, with frameless balanced droplights and lozenge-shaped toplights. These toplights were perhaps the most distinctive feature of Bulleid carriages, steam and electric; quite pleasing on a coach with only three doors each side, but most undesirable when repeated to excess, as on the electric suburban stock with eight or ten doors per side. Certainly sets 963-80 were the closest in appearance to the '4-SUB' electric stock, at least when viewed from the compartment side. On the corridor side, a door was placed opposite each alternate compartment.

Third Brakes in sets 963-80 were numbered 2841 to 2876: 2841-4 were completed in November 1945; 2845-66 in December; 2867-70 in January 1946; and 2871-6 in February 1946. They seated 40 passengers each, and weighed

32 tons. Composites were numbered 5709 to 5726, Nos. 5713/4/21/5 being completed in February 1946; 5709-12/5-20/2/3 in March; and 5724/6 in April 1946. They seated 24 first- and 24 third-class passengers and weighed 33 tons each.

As the Third Brakes were built in advance of the Composites, they had to be stored until the Composites were ready. One can imagine the difficulty in forming the sets with all coaches in numerical order, but nevertheless this was done with complete success.

These sets were followed by four more in June and July, 1946, to the same Order Number. Coaches forming them were similar in style, but 'stretched', as they had 63 ft 5 in. underframes and a body length of 64 ft 6 in. - now the standard length for SR steam stock. The Third Brakes had six compartments and a slightly smaller luggage compartment; Composites were given an extra third-class compartment (four firsts, four thirds) and the lavatory compartment at each end was made smaller. Otherwise the appearance was similar to that of the 59 ft stock, and it needed a keen eye to distinguish one of these uncommon sets from the more ubiquitous short-bodied stock. Set numbers were 981 to 984, comprising Third Brakes 2877 to 2884 and Composites 5727 to 5730 in numerical order; sets 981/2 appeared in June and 983/4 in July, 1946.

The new trains were put into service on the Waterloo-West of England route. From 7th October, 1946, the following weekday train services were booked to include a '3 corridor set (New)' -

| | |
|---|---|
| Down: | 9.0 am to Plymouth, 9.0 am to Ilfracombe. |
| | 10.50 am to Ilfracombe, 10.50 am to Plymouth. |
| | 11.54 am to Salisbury. |
| | 12.50 pm to Plymouth, 12.50 pm to Ilfracombe. |
| | 2.50 pm to Ilfracombe, 2.50 pm to Plymouth. |
| | 3.20 pm to Bournemouth West. |
| | 3.33 pm to Salisbury (Sats. only). |
| | 4.54 pm (Sats. only) to Basingstoke. |
| | 6.0 pm to Plymouth, 6.0 pm to Exeter Central. |
| | 7.35 pm to Yeovil (Sats. excepted). |
| | |
| Up: | 6.35 am from Basingstoke (Mondays only). |
| | 7.21 am from Bournemouth West. |
| | 7.10 am from Yeovil (forms 11.54 am Down). |
| | 7.30 am from Exeter Central. |
| | 11.50 am (Sats. excepted) from Salisbury. |
| | 8.15 am from Plymouth (one set) and Ilfracombe (one set). |
| | 11.38 am (Sats. only) from Salisbury (forms 3.33 pm Down). |
| | 2.22 pm from Salisbury (forms 4.54 pm Down Sats.) |
| | 10.15 am from Ilfracombe. |
| | 12.15 pm from Ilfracombe (one set) and Plymouth (one set). |
| | 2.25 pm from Plymouth (one set) and Ilfracombe (one set). |
| | 3.45 pm from Plymouth. |

By October, 1947, as further new sets entered into service, the 'long' sets 981-4 were transferred to Brighton/Portsmouth to Plymouth workings, the 'short' sets remaining on West of England services. By September, 1949, however, Nos. 981-4 were back on the main line again, where they remained, some attempt being made to keep them, and 963-80, on stopping services because they compared so unfavourably with later Bulleid stock with its large 'picture' windows. Nos. 963-84 also appeared on Bournemouth, Weymouth, Basingstoke and Salisbury local trains.

By mid-1950s, some sets had been repainted in BR standard crimson lake and cream livery; and in 1957 some were used briefly on Hampshire local services as the diesel-electric trains intended for these were not ready in time; the more frequent services could be worked only by bringing in extra stock. All were in green again by about 1960.

From November 1959, Nos. 963 to 973 were allocated to the Somerset & Dorset line, replacing Maunsell corridor sets, which stood spare; however, from June 1960 the Bulleid stock was needed for the intensive mainline summer services and the pre-war sets returned to the S & D. In 1961 it was found possible to re-allocate the sets for a longer period: Nos. 963 to 972 went to the Somerset & Dorset line; 973 to 979 were transferred to the Central Division for Oxted Line, Reading-Tonbridge, and Brighton-Horsham services; and 980 to 984 were retained for Waterloo-West of England services. Electrification, the withdrawal of older stock, and the 'cascading' of newer stock made this possible.

First alterations to set formations were made in June 1962, when Nos. 980 to 984 were strengthened to eight cars, each with an extra corridor composite and four Maunsell corridor seconds. A year later, sets 973, 978 and 979 were similarly strengthened; at the same time, Nos. 974, 975 and 976 were made up to five coaches with three Maunsell corridor seconds each.

The 1945/6 stock was the first of the Bulleid design to suffer blanket withdrawal, and this occurred in December, 1963: before then, only three Bulleid carriages had been condemned. Sets 963/5/6/9-72/4/5/7-9 were deleted and the vehicles condemned; additionally, sets 973/82/3 were disbanded, 2862/79-82 being condemned and 2861 going to set 984 to replace 2883, which was condemned. Composite 5713 in set 967 was also withdrawn in December 1963, being replaced by 5719 ex 973. Sets remaining in 1964 were 964, 967, 968, 976, 980, 981 and 984; Composites 5727-30 were downgraded to Seconds and renumbered 1727 to 1730. Formations of these sets from 15th June, 1964, was officially as shown below.

| | 964 | 967 | 968 | 976 | 980 | 981 | 984 |
|---|---|---|---|---|---|---|---|
| 2nd Bke | 2843 | 2849 | 2851 | 2867 | 2875 | 2877 | 2861 |
| Second | 1829* | 47† | 51† | 46† | 1206* | 1727 | 1730 |
| Second | 1728 | 1932 | 52† | 48† | 1729 | 1852* | 1194* |
| Compo. | 5710 | 5719 | 5714 | 5722 | 5874† | 5884† | 5897† |
| Compo. | 5907† | 5900† | 5885† | 5751† | 5726† | 5868† | 5872† |
| Second | 1837* | 1933† | 53† | 49† | 1236* | 1192* | 1863* |
| Second | 1235* | 1934† | 55† | 39† | 1208* | 1890* | 1917* |
| 2nd Bke. | 2844 | 2850 | 2852 | 2868 | 2876 | 2878 | 2884 |

* Maunsell vehicle.
† Details of Bulleid Compos and Seconds will be found in later Sections.

Alterations made to sets by 14th June, 1965: 964-1829, 1837 and 1235 replaced by Bulleid Seconds 90, 92 and 31. 980-1206, 1236 and 1208 replaced by Bulleid Seconds 85, 86 and 87. 981-1852, 1192 and 1890 replaced by Bulleid Seconds 34, 35 and 36. 984-1194, 1863 and 1917 replaced by Bulleid Seconds 38, 40 and 41.

Allocation was shown as Waterloo-Salisbury, Waterloo-Bournemouth-Weymouth, and 'Through services to other Regions'. All seven sets lasted until about the end of 1965, and were then disbanded. Second Brake 2850 was withdrawn in November 1965, and was converted into a weedkilling staff coach, No. CWT 13, for the Chipman Chemical Co. based at Horsham.

## THE PROTOTYPE CORRIDOR COMPOSITE

The first post-War 3-coach sets had not shown very much advance on pre-War design, but the Southern's next carriage certainly did. Completed in September, 1945, it was a Composite, No. 5751, with four first-class compartments seating 24 and three third-class compartments with eight seats in each. Instead of doors leading directly into the compartments, there were transverse vestibules with doors at each end of the coach, as well as one between the groups of first- and third-class compartments. The object of this centre vestibule was the easier entraining and detraining of passengers.

Body length was 64 ft 6 in., an increase of 5 ft 6 in. on the pre-War standard; but care in design and construction resulted in a tare weight of no more than 34 tons. Length over headstocks was 63 ft 5 in., and body length over corner pillars 1 in. more. Standard SR 8 ft-wheelbase bogies were fitted, and bogie centres were 46 ft 6 in. Body width was 9 ft, but as the bodyside was a continuous curve from cantrail to floor, with the walls being somewhat thinner than those of Maunsell coaches, the internal width was 3 in. greater at waist level. Height from rail to top of roof was 12 ft 4 1/2 in.

Each compartment had a large fixed window with radiused corners at the base; above it were small rectangular sliding ventilators, the frames of

which were unpainted. The numerals '1' and '3' were located on the respective end doors, not centrally, but close to the door handles; the central doors had no class designation. The word 'SOUTHERN' was placed under the innermost first-class compartment window.

Compartments had hammock-sprung seating frames, with plenty of space under the seats for stowing luggage; electrically-heated foot-warming panels were provided under the floorings (in addition to normal steamheaters); ventilation was provided by an air-duct in the upper part of the corridor partition with which roof torpedo extractors were connected, an air grille being fitted in each compartment over the corridor doorway. The compartments were decorated with polished veneers and fittings such as door-latches, luggage-rack brackets, ash-trays, and corridor handrails were of stainless steel. Mirrors were canted out of the vertical to reduce reflection from the diffused electric lighting.

Compartment-corridor doors were fitted with interlocking brushes to reduce draughts, and in the corridor itself were to be found electrical direction indicators showing 'firsts', 'thirds', and lavatories.

The Southern, having oiled its public relations and publicity machine, was certainly not going to keep this fine new vehicle under its hat, and in any case it needed to know before going ahead with production batches whether the coach would be liked by the public. And so, No. 5751 was placed on exhibition for three days at Waterloo, and again at Victoria during early October, 1945; the public being invited to inspect and criticise the new features of design.

On entering the coach, each person was handed a questionnaire headed 'A New Carriage - Tell us what you think of it'. Spaces were provided marked 'What I like' and 'What I don't like'; and some 2,000 of the estimated 25,000 visitors took the trouble to record their opinions.

Most passengers expressed a preference for compartments rather than open saloons; they wanted individual bracket lamps in both first- and third-class compartments; communication cord to be provided in corridors and lavatories as well as compartments;heating in corridors and lavatories; and the lavatory ventilation to be improved (the frosted glass fitted to the lavatories of No. 5751 had in fact no ventilation at all). All these requirements were noted, and the features were incorporated in the later 'production' 3-coach sets. However, no drastic structural alterations were made to the production Composites; so, had anyone suggested that the lavatory should be located, for example, with two first-class compartments on each side, or that there should be three firsts and four thirds in the coach, these suggestions would presumably have been ignored.

No. 5751 was then displayed in Ashford (Kent) station yard from 13th October, 1945, for a week. Also lined up for inspection were locomotive No. 21 C 111 , and Sherman, Crusader and other tanks.

Eventually the coach went into traffic, being formed temporarily in Set 980 in place of 5726; when the Third Brakes of Set 770, 4301/2, were ready in November, 1947, 5751 was placed permanently in this set. It is believed that its non-standard features, such as the sliding ventilators and lavatory windows, were later altered to match those of the Third Brakes; but certain internal dimensions, and position of lavatory access doors, differed from the 'production' composites and remained so (see diagrams). 5751 stayed in Set 770 until 1964, when it was placed in augmented Set 976 until the final disbanding of Bulleid sets in March, 1966. Withdrawal took place in July, 1967.

## INTRODUCTION OF FIRST 3-COACH SETS 'L'

In January, 1947, *The Southern Railway Magazine* announced that a series of 24 3-coach sets was under construction, half of which would be completed in time for the summer and the other half by the end of the year. Each set consisted of two Third Brakes, each with compartment and saloon seating; and one Composite, with the same layout and seating capacity as the prototype of 1945. The first set, No. 771, was put into service on the 'Atlantic Coast Express' during December, 1946. Of a total of 144 seats, 80 were in compartments (including 24 first-class) and 64 in saloons. This meant that third-class passengers found rather more open saloon seats than their 3-to-1 vote for compartments might have expected them to find; perhaps this was the start of the philosophy that if you want the privacy of compartments you must expect to pay for it!

Each Third Brake had a guard's and luggage compartment, with a set of double doors each side and outward-opening door for the guard. A single periscope was fitted. Next came two compartments, with side corridor on the left-hand side as one looked away from the luggage compartment. Then came a lavatory, rather unusually in the middle of the coach; the longitudinal wall of this compartment was recessed about 1 ft 3 in. from the corridor wall and the space used to store tables, with a switch cabinet above them. The narrow lavatory window had tiny sliding ventilators. A transverse vestibule, with external doors, was located between the lavatory and a 4-bay open saloon, with two-and-two facing seats and a central walkway; finally a further transverse vestibule with external doors was at the inner end of the coach. Tare weight:- 33 tons.

Every large window had all four corners radiused, and included two sliding ventilators at the top. It appears that some sets went into traffic with temporary glass in the ventilators as the makers of the sliding frames could not supply immediately; and each window had a hood presumably bolted on temporarily to prevent rain penetration.

Overall dimensions of both types of coach in the sets were the same as

those given for the prototype; the chief internal alteration in the Composites was that the lavatory access doors opened from the transverse vestibules at each end of the coach, instead of from the corridor. As in the Third Brakes, switch cabinets and portable table storage were located in the alcove between each end compartment and lavatory compartment, facing the corridor.

The sets included the following features which had been suggested by passengers in the 1945 questionnaire:—

> Individual bracket lamps in both first- and third-class compartments, in addition to general roof lighting;
> Passenger communication cord in compartments, corridors and lavatories;
> Heaters for corridors and lavatories;
> Two heaters in every first-class compartment, one under each seat, the heat being controlled by passengers.

As with No. 5751, the vehicles had curved sides, giving an extra 3 in. for seating space; and the seats were hammock-sprung, with insert cushions, and with space underneath for luggage (and also to save weight and facilitate cleaning).

Third Brakes were numbered 4301 to 4348, and were formed in order and in numerical pairs in Sets 770 to 793; Composites were Nos. 5752 to 5774, in Sets 771 to 793 in order. The 1945 Composite, 5751, was placed in Set 770.

Official dates of completion of the sets are:

| | | | | | | |
|---|---|---|---|---|---|---|
| 771-4: | Dec. 1946 | 784: | Apr. 1947 | 789-92: | Oct. 1947 |
| 775/6: | Jan. 1947 | 785-7: | May 1947 | 770: | Nov. 1947 |
| 777-80: | Feb. 1947 | 788: | June 1947 | 793: | Nov. 1947 |
| 781-3: | Mar. 1947 | Order No. 3235. | | | |

It was settled that the '1' and '3' class numerals should appear not on the doors, but beside them, aligned about mid-way between the bottom of the window ventilators and the base of the large fixed pane. On the Composites, this had the advantage that the centre door had '1' on one side of it and '3' on the other, indicating to the passenger which way to turn when he entered the carriage. On Third Brakes, 'SOUTHERN' appeared under the saloon window adjacent to the centre door.

In the Carriage Working Notices, Sets 770-793 were designated 'L', although this indication was for working purposes only and was not really meant to be taken as a classification letter. In the notice for 6.10.47, it was stressed that these new sets must not work off the SR, and were to be used only in the services shown; these included Waterloo-Bournemouth-Weymouth, and Waterloo-West of England.

First set to be repainted was 788, which was chosen to wear British Railways' experimental 'plum and spilt milk' livery - colours which looked

fine when new, but which weathered horribly. Incidentally, the name of this colour scheme was the official one, improbable though it might seem. In 1949, crimson lake and cream became the standard livery for mainline carriages, and several 3-sets 'L' were repainted in this style; then in spring 1956 came the British Transport Commission's decision to abandon crimson and cream and adopt green for all Southern Region carriages.

Small modifications made over the years were the replacement of the two short handrails beside the guard's door by one long handrail; and the removal of the uppermost roof rainstrip of the two each side that were originally provided. Standardisation was never achieved; the rainstrips were removed on a haphazard basis from about 1952, presumably when the roofs needed re-canvassing; and even in 1967 several coaches still had their upper rainstrips in place.

From 1954, the restriction barring Bulleid stock from working off the Southern was lifted. The 3-sets 'L', which were joined by many others to a slightly different design but with the same layout and seating capacity, remained for the whole of their time on the Weymouth and West of England services, and none was allocated to any specific train service; a set formed one day in a fast train might well find itself next day in a local train from Ilfracombe to Exeter or Exeter to Salisbury.

During the summer seasons, some sets in the 770-793 series were strengthened to five coaches, two corridor thirds being added; but this was never done on a regular basis as were the later sets 830-849. Set 793, for example, was running with extra thirds in April, 1956: it was freshly painted in crimson and cream. The Thirds were also painted in those colours. Ultimately, all sets were painted B.R. green.

First withdrawals were of sets 772 (April 1964) and 782 (May 1964). Also in 1964, set 770 was re-formed (the only one of the series that was). Composite No. 5751 was removed and placed in set 976, and a B.R. open first, S3504, and seven Bulleid open seconds were formed into the set. It was then kept for special traffic on the South Western Division.

Later in 1964, several sets were disbanded, the second brakes in most cases being transferred to the Western Region and the composites condemned. Presumably the Western did not care very much for its acquisitions, as most were condemned only a few months after receipt. Although at this time the WR was responsible for all the former SR lines west of Wilton, all carriages working to and from Waterloo were still Southern, only local services in the West using WR stock (or ex-SR carriages with 'W'-prefixes to the numbers). So quite possibly the Southern Region, which was busily running down its fleet of carriages, thought the Western might like to have some modern Bulleid stock to replace the elderly Maunsell coaches with which it had been lumbered on 1st January, 1963.

Second brakes transferred were 4307-9 (11/64); 4311/2/7/8 (1/65); 4319/20/7/8 (11/64); 4329/30 (10/64); 4331/2 (1/65); and 4339/40 (11/64), following the disbanding of sets 773/4/5/8/9/83-5/9.

4310 from set 774 was retained by the Southern as a loose coach; the composites were condemned in October 1964 (5756, 5770) and November 1964 (5754, 5755, 5759, 5760, 5764 and 5765). Additionally, set 791 was disbanded early in 1965, the Second Brakes going to loose stock and the Composite being withdrawn in February. This left sets 771, 776, 777, 780, 781, 786 to 788, 790, 792 and 793 still intact and with their original formations, which were maintained until about March, 1966, when all sets were officially disbanded and set numbers painted out.

## THE BOURNEMOUTH DINING SETS

These eleven 6-coach sets, intended specifically for Waterloo-Bournemouth services, were the first truly-integrated dining sets to be built by the Southern; previous practice had always been to marshall loose restaurant cars and open thirds in the middle of the permanent sets, and to remove them if required. But with these new trains, the kitchen and dining cars were part of the set, and accordingly bore set numbers.

Great care was also taken in the layout of the individual coaches, and the positioning of third-class compartments and saloons, first-class compartments and saloon; and of lavatories, so that no passenger had to walk too far to gain access to one.

Each set was made up of: 1 semi-open third brake, to same design as 4301 etc.; 1 corridor composite, to same design as 5752 etc., and with third-class end next to third brake; 1 first, with three compartments and a 4-bay dining saloon, the compartment end being next to the compo; 1 kitchen and third-class dining saloon, the kitchen being adjacent to the saloon end of the First; 1 8-bay Open Third, with two lavatories at one end; and 1 semi-saloon third brake.

Like the 3-coach sets, these had many of the features first seen in the prototype coach of 1945: curved bodysides and window glass; heated corridors and lavatories; hammock-sprung compartment seating with insert cushions; and electrically-heated foot-mats between the compartment seats, fitted under the floor covering.

Doors were pressed steel with frameless balanced drop lights and were described as 'light'; though in later years one writer who was working on the restoration of similar coaches referred to 'Mr. Bulleid's heavy, rust-accumulating, steel doors'.

The first-class saloon had loose chairs, floral-patterned, for 24 diners (four tables, each for four passengers, on one side of the walkway; and four

tables, each for two, on the other side). Afterwards, the three first class compartments were provided with tables to allow for 18 extra dining seats. Fluorescent light was installed in the saloon; to avoid projection into the car, the fittings were recessed into the ceilings, the light passing through a 'reeded' glass. Table lamps with separate switches were fixed to a rail which ran along the bodyside, and were supplied from the battery through a control switch in the corridor. There were wall-pictures between each window, and the floor was carpeted.

Said *The Southern Railway Magazine*: 'Kitchen units have been designed to ensure that meals are prepared in the most hygienic and up-to-date conditions possible during the train journey'[1]. Originally, oil gas was supplied; in later years, Propane gas. This provided heat for a double oven, the doors of which were made in two flap portions; a double insulated griller and salamander (a hot iron plate for browning omelettes etc.); an automatically-filled water-fed steamer; and a thermostatically-controlled water heater for washing-up water. In addition to the cooking unit, there was a boiling pan-cum-frier for vegetables and fish frying. In the adjacent pantry were a refrigerator and a mechanically cooled ice cream conservator. At the end of the car a compartment and lavatory were provided for use by the kitchen and pantry staff.

The dining saloon in the kitchen car comprised eight tables with four loose chairs at each - 32 seats. As in the first-class saloon, there were table lamps (fixed to the walls and not actually the tables themselves); and curtains to the windows.

The open third coach, which was fitted with tables, had a transverse vestibule at one end, a 4-bay saloon with 32 seats, a centre vestibule, another 32-seat saloon, a transverse vestibule, and two lavatories adjoining a centre corridor at the other end of the coach, adjacent to the third brake coach.

Externally, the most noticeable feature of the coaches which distinguished them from the earlier sets was that the steel bodysides were extended down to the bottom of the solebars, except where stepboards were positioned; this somehow gave the carriages a particularly opulent air. Coach ends were painted green, except those of the first set; this again had never been done before and, with the gleaming chromium-plated handrails, helped to give the sets their superbly luxurious appearance.

---

1 *Southern Railway Magazine*, Vol. 25, p. 129

The sets, which were numbered 290 to 300, were built and formed as follows:-

ORDER No. 3234

|            | 290     | 291     | 292      | 293      |
|------------|---------|---------|----------|----------|
| Thd Bke    | 4349    | 4351    | 4353     | 4355     |
| Compo      | 5740    | 5741    | 5742     | 5743     |
| Res 1st    | 7677    | 7678    | 7679     | 7680     |
| Res Kitch. | 7881    | 7882    | 7883     | 7884     |
| Open Thd   | 1451    | 1452    | 1453     | 1454     |
| Thd Bke    | 4350    | 4352    | 4354     | 4356     |
|            |         |         |          |          |
| Built      | 8. 1947 | 9. 1947 | 10. 1947 | 10. 1947 |

ORDER No. 3240

|            | 294      | 295      | 296     | 297     |
|------------|----------|----------|---------|---------|
| Thd Bke    | 4357     | 4359     | 4361    | 4363    |
| Compo      | 5744     | 5745     | 5746    | 5747    |
| Res 1st    | 7681     | 7682     | 7683    | 7684    |
| Res Kitch. | 7885     | 7886     | 7887    | 7888    |
| Open Thd.  | 1455     | 1456     | 1457    | 1458    |
| Thd Bke    | 4358     | 4360     | 4362    | 4364    |
|            |          |          |         |         |
| Built      | 12. 1947 | 12. 1947 | 1. 1948 | 1. 1948 |

|            | 298     | 299     | 300     |
|------------|---------|---------|---------|
| Thd Bke    | 4365    | 4367    | 4369    |
| Compo      | 5748    | 5749    | 5750    |
| Res 1st    | 7685    | 7686    | 7687    |
| Res Kitch. | 7889    | 7890    | 7891    |
| Open Thd   | 1459    | 1460    | 1461    |
| Thd Bke    | 4366    | 4368    | 4370    |
|            |         |         |         |
| Built      | 2. 1948 | 2. 1948 | 3. 1948 |

Total seating capacity in each set was 66 first- and 216 third-class; or 42 first- and 184 third-class, excluding dining seats. Third brakes weighed 33 tons each, composites 34 tons, and open thirds 32 tons.

The first train was brought into service on the Bournemouth line in September, 1947, immediately gaining the approval of the popular Press, who acclaimed it as 'The Dream Train'. It was unfortunate that the sets were not ready in time for the summer services - which began on 16 June - especially as there were 450 fewer steam coaches in use than before the War; but 'new ones are being turned out as fast as lack of skilled labour and materials permit'; 1 so really the SR's efforts in producing these magnificent coaches in

1 *Southern Railway Magazine*, Vol 25, p. 129

such difficult conditions were heroic.

Underframes and bogies, which were built at Lancing, were of standard design, except that instead of being equipped with two 22-in. diameter vacuum brake cylinders with brake shafts they had one Westinghouse Brake & Signal Co. 'Prestall' vacuum brake lever cylinder of 30 in. diameter. The object was to reduce weight, and it was hoped it would need less maintenance; subsequently, however, many were re-fitted with two sets of brakegear with the single reservoir left intact except on the kitchen thirds.

When in 1948 BR was experimenting with liveries, set 299 was chosen for painting in 'plum and spilt milk'; also painted in this livery were 3-set 'L' 788, and Maunsell corridor thirds 1200,1254, and corridor first 7224. These were used on the 7.20 am Bournemouth West to Waterloo and the 3.30 pm Down: the formation of the 3.30 was 3-set 'L', 6 dining set, 3 loose coaches. This livery lasted until about 1954, when replaced presumably by carmine and cream. Other sets also appeared in this livery, but from 1956/7 repaints were in B.R. green - a shade darker than S.R. malachite.

During the whole of their existence, sets 290-300 worked on the Bournemouth line and occasionally to Weymouth, but never to Exeter, so far as can be ascertained. In the summer seasons during the 1950s, they usually included some extra loose coaches, and all eleven sets were diagrammed for working. During the winter timetable, however, two sets stood spare; clearly it was only within this period that heavy overhauls could be carried out.

In 1960, set 290 was made up to a 7 dining set by adding a BR open second, and was used on the 8.20 am Waterloo to Bournemouth West and 12.20 pm return, Mondays to Fridays. It reverted to its original six coaches in 1961.

The first alterations of a permanent nature were the removal, from June 1962, of the Kitchen/Dining cars and substitution of new BR buffet/ restaurant cars from the S1716-24 and S1755-72 series. Nos. 7881-8 were condemned officially in January 1964, although Southern Carriage & Wagon Society observers had noted 7881, 7883 and 7888 as branded with condemnation saltires as early as July 1963. Nos. 7889 to 7891 were retained a little longer, being withdrawn in June and July, 1965.

Alterations to the sets from late 1963 on are shown below.

290: 5740 to loose, repl. by First 7647 ex 804, 1964. Set wdn. by 2/65; 4349/50 to 212, 7647 wdn. 2/65, 7677 to 294,1451 to loose.

291: Set wdn. by 6/64. 4351 to 805, 4352 to 865, 5741 to 769, 7678 to loose, 1452 to 770.

292: Set wdn. by 6/64. 4353/4 to 212, 5742 to loose, 7679 to loose, 1453 to 212.

293: Reduced to 3-set, with 4355/6 and 5743. 7680 to loose, 1454 to 885, 6/64.

294: 5744 wdn 2/65, repl. by 5808 ex loose, 7681 wdn. 3/65, repl. by7677 ex 290.

295: Set wdn by 12/63. 4359/60, 5745, wdn. 5/64; 7682 wdn. 12/63, 1456 to 212.

296: Set wdn. by 4/64. 4361 to 237, 4362 wdn. 4/64, 5746 wdn. 5/64, 7683 to loose, to 297 6/65, 1457 to 212.

297:   7684 wdn. 11/64, repl. by 7683 ex loose, ex 296.
298:   4365/6 to loose, 6/65, repl. by BR cor. bke. compos. S21268/9. 7685 wdn.
       2/65, repl. by BR open second S3921.
299:   4367 to loose, 6/65, repl. by BR cor. bke. compo. S21266. 4368 to 952, 6/65,
       repl. by 4358 ex 294, 5749 to loose, 7686 wdn. 1/65, 1460 to loose, not
       replaced. 7648 and BR open second S3941 added, 6/65.
300:   4369/70 to loose, 6/65, repl. by BR cor. bke. compos. S21272/3. 7687 wdn.
       3/65, repl. by BR open 2nd S3833, 1461 to loose, repl. by 1481.

All these altered sets, with the exception of 293, continued work on the
Bournemouth line. 293, now a 3-set 'L', joined the other 3-sets 'L' working in
West of England and Weymouth services.

Of the dining firsts, all had been withdrawn by March 1965 except 7677
and 7683. No. 7679 was sold to the Sadler Rail Coach Co. in 1965, and was
kept at Droxford on the closed Meon Valley line until it was burnt in about
1968. No. 7684 was altered to a Composite Diner by 1964, retaining 1st-class
seating in the three compartments but with 24 2nd-class seats in the saloon.

All remaining sets were disbanded by early 1966.

## 2-COACH SETS 'R' AND LOOSE STOCK

For the West of England services, loose composite brakes and two-coach
sets each formed of a third brake and compo brake had been provided for
many years; and in 1948 thirteen new 2-coach sets were constructed as direct
replacements of most of the Maunsell stock, some of which was relegated to
local services in the Western District.

Each new set comprised one semi-saloon third brake, identical to those in
3-sets 770-793 except that the stepboards outside the guard's and luggage
compartments were 15 ft 6 1/2in. long instead of 16 ft 4 in.; and one corridor
brake composite, with four third-class compartments and two first-class.
Layout comprised a rather small luggage and guard's compartment, only 14
ft 8 3/4in. long and nearly 2 ft shorter than those provided in the third brakes;
two first-class compartments; external doors with transverse vestibule; four
third-class compartments; lavatory; and transverse vestibule and external
doors at the inner end. Corridor was on the left-hand side when viewed
from the van.

Set numbers were 63 to 75, and coaches were allocated in numerical
order:  Third Brakes 4371 to 4383, and Compo Brakes 6700 to 6712.
Constructions dates are:

| | | | | | |
|---|---|---|---|---|---|
| 4371-4 | March 1948 | 4375-80 | April 1948 | 4381-3 | May1948 |
| 6700-2 | March 1948 | 6703-8 | April 1948 | 6709-12 | May 1948 |

All the sets were in traffic by June, 1948. Livery was Southern Railway malachite, but the word 'Southern' was omitted; coach numbers appeared in the upper position at each end as before, but were prefixed by 'S'. It is believed that set numbers were also painted with an 'S' prefix, and sets 63 and 66, at least, displayed this style, which did not last long. Order Nos. 3236 (sets 63-6), 3242 (67-9), 3244 (70/1), and 3252 (72-5).

Sets 63 to 75 were allocated to Waterloo-West of England services for the whole of their time and, so far as can be established, never strayed from these workings. The sets were kept intact until the first withdrawals, which were in 1964 when Nos. 64, 65, 67, 71, 74 and 75 were deleted. In 1965, those remaining had the Brake Second removed and replaced by Corridor Second coaches, as shown.

| | |
|---|---|
| 27 to set 63, ex Loose. | 91 to set 70, ex Loose. |
| 112 to set 68, ex set 80. | 105 to set 72, ex Loose. |
| 43 to set 69, ex Loose | 98 to set 73, ex Loose. |

Set 66 meanwhile was strengthened to include later Bulleid composite 5916 and a BR miniature buffet car for use on Waterloo-Exeter services. The 2-sets 'R' no longer had any work in the West of England as trains now terminated at Exeter, and all sets were disbanded by March, 1966.

Later in 1948, several loose coaches were put into traffic: forty brake composites, for single through-carriage working between Waterloo and the West of England: five corridor thirds; and 13 corridor composites. The brake compos intended for loose working had a different layout from those formed in 2-sets 'R': the lavatory was in the centre, as if to emphasise the self-contained nature of the coach. Accommodation comprised guard's and luggage compartment, 14 ft 8 3/4 in. long; two first-class compartments; transverse vestibule; lavatory compartment; four third-class compartments; and vestibule at the end. Corridor was on the left-hand side when viewed from the guard's compartment, which was equipped with two periscopes because one never knew which way round in the train the brake-end would be, and the guard would therefore need facilities to see along the train in either direction.

Numbers of the loose brake composites were 6713 to 6752; Nos. 6713-33 were built in August, 1948, and the remainder in September, to three Order Numbers: 3237 (6713-30), 3247 (6731/2), and 3256 (6733-52).

The five corridor thirds, which were built in late 1948, were Nos. 1932 to 1936, and had the same window and door layout as the open thirds in the 6-dining sets; like them they had two lavatory compartments at one end, divided by a short centre corridor. There were eight compartments, seating a total of 64 passengers; the corridor was on the right-hand side when viewed from the lavatory end of the coach. (Order No. 3254.)

Finally, the loose corridor composites, which all came out in September, 1948 (built to Order No. 3255), were similar in appearance to the compos in Sets 771-793, but had much shorter stepboards to the doors. The boards for the extreme right hand doors (when viewed from either side) were only 2 ft 5 3/4 in. long, whereas those in the same position on composites 5752-74 were 4 ft 11 1/2 in. Coach numbers of the loose composites were 5799 to 5811. Order Nos. 3246 (5799-5802), and 3255 (5803-11).

All three types appeared in Southern livery, without the word 'Southern'; with prefix 'S' to coach numbers; and probably without the class indication '3' on the bodyside.

In 1951, a 4-coach set, No. 400, for Waterloo-Exeter services, was formed from examples of the loose stock just described: Compo Brake 6728, Compo 5803, Third 1934, Compo Brake 6738. This ran until late 1959, when 5803 was transferred to 8-set 206 and the three other vehicles reverted to loose stock. The only other loose brake compo to go to a set before 1964 was 6713, which with Brake Second 4282 formed an additional 2-set 'R', No. 76, from 1960 until November, 1964. One or two loose brakes compos were repainted in BR crimson lake and cream, but in most cases the malachite lasted until 1956/7, when BR green became standard.

All the Thirds and Compos eventually found themselves in sets, but these tended to be short-lived.

With the transfer to the Western Region from 1st January, 1963, of all Southern lines in the West of England, several ex-Southern coaches found themselves under new management. Most of the carriages transferred were pre-war corridors, but some Bulleid vehicles went too; these were loose composite brakes Nos. 6714-17, 6719, 6726 and 6738. They were followed by 6742 and 6746 in November, 1964. The Western operated these ex-Southern vehicles for two or three years after taking them over; the Southern, however-er, withdrew its first examples of the type during 1964: 6713/8/20/4/5/8/30-3/7/9/40/3-5/48-52. For summer, 1964, Nos. 6725 and 6735, and Composite 5802, were formed with seven Maunsell Corridor Seconds into 10 set 952, for Margate-Wolverhampton services. By June, 1965, this had become a 4-set, Second Brake 4368 ex set 299 replacing 6725, a BR miniature buffet car being included, and all the Maunsell coaches scrapped. This, like the re-formed set 66, was used on Waterloo-Salisbury-Exeter ser-vices - probably the 11.0 am Down, which now terminated at Salisbury, and the 5.0 pm Waterloo-Exeter.

Loose brake composites withdrawn in 1965 were 6721-3 and 6747, so that all that remained at the end of 1965 were 6727, 6729, 6734, 6735, 6736 and 6741. In contrast, only one of the Composites had gone by that time - 5805; and the corridor seconds, 1932-6, were intact.

Three sets were made up in 1965 for the reduced Waterloo-Exeter service:

two of 8 corridors and one of 7, each including a Kitchen Buffet car. Only the Second Brakes were Bulleid coaches, spare after the alteration of 2-sets 63, 68 to 70, 72, and 73. 8-set 701 had 4371 and 4381; 8-set 702 had 4376 and 4377; and 7-set 703, 4378 and 4380. Other vehicles were BR Standards.

## CONTRACTOR-BUILT SETS

Overlapping the introduction of the last examples of small-ventilator stock and the first of the large-ventilator carriages came 35 three-coach sets built by Birmingham Railway Carriage & Wagon Co. at Smethwick. The vehicles making up these sets were so different in appearance from those of the Eastleigh-built stock - indeed, some features were retrograde - that it seems probable that the design preceded that of the 1945 Prototype and its offspring.

Because of lack of materials, the Southern was unable to construct the sets itself; consequently, it was forced to turn to an outside contractor. But these manufacturers were also subject to rigid controls on the amount of material they could use; the Ministry of War Transport 'allocated capacity' in the shops of outside contractors to railway companies requiring new stock, effectively making the railways wait their turn and causing lengthy delay in the fulfilment of orders.

At last, by November, 1945, the SR had been allocated capacity in the shops for construction of 72 coaches in 1946, and the tender of Birmingham Railway Carriage & Wagon Co. was considered for 24 3-coach sets for a maximum cost of £456,000, 'subject to price variation and cost investigation clauses and to the consent of the Minister of War Transport. The Ministry had agreed that the Exchequer should, as a special arrangement, bear the excess of current contractors' prices over railway shop costs.'

Two months later, the SR was given permission to order 18 more coaches in 1946, and so the Company asked BRC&W to increase its quotation to include six additional 3-car sets at a similar price and subject to the same conditions. By February the tender had been accepted: Smethwick was to construct and supply 30 3-coach sets for £570,000, or £19,000 per set.

None was completed in 1946, but in July the SR was allocated capacity in the shops of outside contractors for construction in 1947 of a further 15 vehicles, and the Ministry of Transport had consented to this. Orders were then placed with BRC&W for five 3-car sets at the same price and subject to the same conditions as before. These coaches were not in fact delivered until spring 1949.

The first two sets were delivered in December, 1947 and were numbered 795 and 796. They had two unpleasing features. The windows were excessively shallow, the window base being level with the door droplight base;

this, coupled with somewhat 'low-down' seats, meant a passenger's chin was about level with the window-ledge. Secondly, corridor windows had no ventilators at all, and, to the observer outside, this side of the coach presented a 'blank-faced' look which was a little disconcerting. However, so that corridor-walkers should not suffocate, the lack of corridor opening windows was balanced by much larger air intakes on the roof. Compartment windows had shallow sliding ventilators incorporating a type of 'baffle' which was claimed to be draughtproof. Overall dimensions of BRC&W coaches were the same as Eastleigh types, but internal dimensions, and layout of the Third Brakes, differed. The first twenty Third Brakes, Nos. 4209 to 4228 in sets 795 to 804, each had a guard's and luggage compartment 17 ft 3 in. long; a 4-seat coupé compartment and 8-seat ordinary compartment; transverse vestibule; 4-bay saloon (32 seats); a lavatory compartment opposite which was a space fitted with luggage racks; and a transverse vestibule at the end of the coach. The reason for a coupé compartment is not at all clear; it did give a slightly larger luggage space, but was not perpetuated and Third Brakes built for the remaining sets, 805 to 829, had two 8-seat compartments at the expense of a smaller guard's van, the rest of the coach being the same as Nos. 4209-28. These Third Brakes were numbered 4229, 4230, and 4251 to 4298. Layout of the Composites was the same as that of Nos. 5751 etc., with four 1st-class and three 3rd-class compartments and two lavatories. Compartments were slightly narrower owing to their partitions being slightly thicker. Coach numbers were 5775 to 5798, in sets 795 to 818; and 5812 to 5822, formed in sets 819 to 829.

Official building dates are shown below:—

**Third Brakes**

| | | | | | |
|---|---|---|---|---|---|
| 4209-12 | Dec. 1947 | 4251-4 | Aug. 1948 | 4269-75 | Feb. 1949 |
| 4213/4 | Jan. 1948 | 4255/6 | Sep. 1948 | 4276-82 | Jan. 1949 |
| 4215-22 | Apr. 1948 | 4257-60 | Oct. 1948 | 4283-8 | Feb. 1949 |
| 4223-8 | May 1948 | 4261/2 | Dec. 1948 | 4289-92 | Mar. 1949 |
| 4229/30 | Jul. 1948 | 4263-8 | Jan. 1949 | 4293-8 | Apr. 1949 |

**Composites**

| | | | | | |
|---|---|---|---|---|---|
| 5775/6 | Dec. 1947 | 5786/7 | Sep. 1948 | 5795-7 | Dec. 1948 |
| 5777/8 | Jan. 1948 | 5788-90 | Oct. 1948 | 5812-4 | Jan. 1949 |
| 5779-81 | Mar. 1948 | 5791 | Dec. 1948 | 5815-9 | Feb. 1949 |
| 5782-5 | Jul. 1948 | 5792-4/8 | Jan. 1949 | 5820-2 | Apr. 1949 |

Livery was malachite green, and doubtless the first sets would have been lettered 'Southern'. It is not thought that any were repainted in British Railways crimson lake and cream.

At first, all the sets ran on the Western Section; soon, however, Nos. 795 to 804 (with 44-seat Third Brakes) went to the Eastern where, from

September 1948, they were allocated to London-Dover-Ramsgate-Margate services, and later referred to in the Carriage Working Notices as '3 Cor "M" Sets'. The balance remained on the Western for Waterloo-Weymouth and Waterloo-West of England services as 3-sets 'L', having the same seating capacity as the 1947-built sets 770-793.

The 3-sets 'M' ran on all the best S.E. mainline services, one set usually forming the front part of Down trains such as the 11.15 am, 1.15 and 4.15 pm from Charing Cross; the 4.15 was named 'The Man of Kent' from the start of the summer services in June 1953. Some stock shuffling occurred in June 1954: sets 795 to 802 went to the 'Oxted' group of lines, providing them with their first regular view of Bulleid carriages; and sets 803/4 were disbanded, the stock being re-formed as under:

| Set 473 | Thd Bke | 4225 | Ex 803 |
|---------|---------|------|--------|
|         | Third   | 81   | Ex Loose |
|         | Third   | 82   | Ex Loose |
|         | First   | 7648 | Ex Loose |
|         | Res. Car | -   | - |
|         | Third   | 83   | Ex Loose |
|         | Thd Bke | 4226 | Ex 803 |
| Set 474 | Thd Bke | 4227 | Ex 804 |
|         | Third   | 85   | Ex Loose |
|         | Third   | 86   | Ex Loose |
|         | Compo   | 5783 | Ex 803 |
|         | Compo   | 5784 | Ex 804 |
|         | Third   | 87   | Ex Loose |
|         | Third   | 90   | Ex Loose |
|         | Thd Bke | 4228 | Ex 804 |

Both of these were then allocated to London-Ramsgate (via Chatham) services, and stayed on them until the electrification in June 1959. Set 473 was disbanded, all stock going to Loose; set 474 went to a London-Deal working until September, and then London-Dover-Margate from June 1960. In 1961 it was on the Western Section and in summer 1964 (with corridor second 92 added) it worked a Bournemouth-Sheffield service; stock was finally dispersed at the end of 1964. Incidentally, Third Brakes 4225/6 in set 473 were replaced in June 1955 by BR standard vehicles 34245/6, these remaining until June 1959. 4225/6 went to set 211; then, from June 1958, set 897, formed for Oxted Line workings.

In June 1955, 'M' set 802 was increased to 5 coaches by adding Third 92 and Compo 5887; it was berthed at Forest Row for an Oxted Line service. In November 1956, set 801 was strengthened and 802 altered to match it, in order that both sets could be used on 2-day cycles taking in London-

Tunbridge Wells West-Forest Row.  Formation was now:-

| Set 801 | 2nd Bke | 4221 | |
|---------|---------|------|--|
|         | Second  | 97   | Ex Loose |
|         | First   | 7635 | Ex Loose |
|         | Second  | 98   | Ex Loose |
|         | 2nd Bke | 4222 | |
| | | | |
| Set 802 | 2nd Bke | 4223 | |
|         | Second  | 92   | |
|         | First   | 7630 | Ex Loose |
|         | Second  | 99   | Ex Loose.  Repl. 4/57 by 122 ex Set 279. |
|         | 2nd Bke | 4224 | |

They remained on these services until the diesels started in 1962.  Both of the Compos from sets 801/2, Nos. 5781/2, became Loose stock, and in 1959 were fitted with electric heaters, possibly for use in the 'Night Ferry' electrically-hauled service.

3-sets 'M' continued on general Oxted Line services until June 1959, when they were transferred to the Western Section for the West of England and Weymouth trains.  Meanwhile, set 795 had suffered some damage in (presumably) a shunting accident at Eastbourne on 17th April, 1958, which resulted in the withdrawal of Second Brake 4209; however, the set was not deleted until April, 1959, when 4210 went to set 821, one of whose 2nd Brakes had also been damaged, and 5775 to Loose stock.  Thus, the remaining 3-sets 'M' arriving on the Western Section in 1959 were Nos. 796 to 800.

The 3-sets 'L', Nos. 805-29, which were always on the Western Section, suffered no changes until March 1956, when set 821 was involved in a mishap and 2nd Brake 4281 withdrawn, its underframe going to Lancing Carriage Works for internal use there as No. 080629.  Set 821 ran with a temporary 2nd Brake until April 1959, when 4210 ex set 795 was substituted.  However, a year later the set was disbanded:  4210 to set 433, 5814 to Loose, and 4282 to 2-set 76.

In June 1957, set 805 lost its Compo and was altered to a 6-car buffet set, with First 7622 ex Loose, Bulleid Kitchen Buffet and Restaurant Composite Open, and BR open second 3846; the set then ran on a regular Bournemouth West-Waterloo service for several years.

It should be noted that, during the currency of the summer timetables, from June to September each year, some of these 3-sets were strengthened with two extra Thirds each, none of which was ever stencilled with a set number; during the 'winter', the sets once again reverted to 3-car.  The exceptions were sets 826-9, which from late 1959 became permanent 5-sets with Seconds 106 to 113, allocated in order and in numerical pairs.  They reverted to 3-sets in winter 1962.

From 1963, the Southern's quick and easy method of disposing of surplus carriages not due for scrapping was to dump them on a possibly unwilling Western Region. This was what happened to nearly all the 44-seat BRC&W second brakes, which tended to remain on the former Southern lines west of Salisbury; some lasted until 1968. Those transferred were 4210/1/3-6, 4219-28, all between October 1964 and February 1965, resulting in the disbanding of sets 796-8, 800-2, and 474. 4212 (set 796) was not transferred, but condemned in January 1965; compos. 5776-8 (796-8) and 5783/4 (474) were withdrawn in Nov. 1964 and 5780 (800) in October. Replacement Compos. 5891 (801) and 5878 (802) were both withdrawn in November 1964.

During summer 1964, sets 807-812 ran as 5-sets with two extra corridor seconds each: 50, 83 (807); 84,104 (808);106/7 (809);108/9 (810); 110/1 (811); and 99, 113 (812). All save 808 and 809 had reverted to 3 sets by 1965. Other alterations and withdrawals, 1964/5, were:- 805: 4230 wdn. 4/64, repl. by 4351 ex 291. 806: disbanded 1964, stock to loose (5786 wdn. 11/64). 810: disbanded 1965, stock to loose (5790 wdn. 12/65). 811 : wdn. 3/65, 110/1 to loose. 812: disbanded 1965, stock to loose. 813: disbanded 1965, stock to loose; 5793 wdn. 12/65. 814: wdn. 1964, 4267/8 to loose, 5794 cond. 12/64. 817: 4273, 5797 wdn. 12/65; 4274 to loose. 823: wdn. 5/64. 825: wdn. 2/65. 827: wdn. 1/65. 829: wdn. 4/64. Additionally, Second Brake 4282 (set 76) was transferred to the Western Region in March 1965.

## 4-COACH SETS 'N'

The coaches making up 15 4-coach sets introduced early in 1949 showed one very obvious difference from all the preceding Bulleid 64 ft 6 in. stock; the sliding ventilators on both compartment and corridor windows were much larger, being 15 in. deep instead of only 10 1/4 in. as before. It must have been felt that the narrow ventilators provided inadequate ventilation, as all subsequent new construction had large ventilators as standard; but none of the early stock was ever modified to match. The large ventilators did rather spoil the appearance of the coaches, making them look heavy and 'ordinary'; the earlier version was much more distinctive and Southern-ish.

Other less noticeable differences: guard's door had beside it one long grab handle instead of two short ones; shorter stepboard for guard's and luggage compartment at one side, and separate stepboards under the double doors and guard's door on the other side of the coach; shorter stepboards for passenger doors on Third Brakes and Composites; and corridor handrails fixed slightly lower than those of carriages with small ventilators.

Otherwise, the layout of the coaches (Third Brake, Third, Composite, Third Brake) was the same as that of the 1947/8 Eastleigh-built stock. Set numbers were 80 to 94, and individual cars were numbered 4011 to 4040

(Third Brakes), 26 to 40 (Thirds), and 5823 to 5837 (Composites) all being allocated in numerical order.

Building dates: 26/7/9 - Jan. 1949, 28 - Dec. 1948, 30-5 - Feb. 1949, 30-40 - Mar. 1949.  4011-4 - Jan. 1949, 4015/6 - Dec. 1948, 4017/8 - Jan. 1949, 4019-22 - Feb. 1949, 4023-30 - Jan. 1949, 4031-4 - Feb. 1949, 4035-40 - Mar. 1949. 5823/4/6/9-32 - Jan. 1949, 5825 - Dec. 1948, 5827/8 - Feb. 1949, 5833-7 - Mar. 1949.  Built to Order No. 3249.  Livery was malachite green; at least one set, No. 83, had 'S' prefix.

4-sets 'N' Nos. 80 to 94 were allocated to the Eastern Section from May 1949, for London-Dover-Ramsgate-Margate services, working mostly in semi-fast trains.  No changes were made until June 1959, when the new electric services rendered much stock superfluous; at least two 4-sets 'N' were transferred to the Oxted Line ( normally Nos. 89 and 90 but others did appear from time to time), being berthed at Tunbridge Wells West and East Grinstead.  Set 80 and 86 were strengthened in February 1959, and worked regular London-Dover-Margate trains, such as the 9.10 am down.

| Set 80 | 2nd Bke | 4011 | | Set 86 | 2nd Bke | 4023 |
|--------|---------|------|--|--------|---------|------|
| | Second | 26 | | | Second | 32 |
| | Compo | 5823 | | | Compo | 5829 |
| | Compo | 5884 Ex Loose | | | Compo | 5886 Ex Loose |
| | Open 2nd | 1477 Ex Loose | | | Open 2nd | 1482 Ex Loose |
| | Open 2nd | 1479 Ex Loose | | | Open2nd | 1487 Ex Loose |
| | 2nd Bke | 4012 | | | 2nd Bke | 4024 |

These formations were maintained until the second stage of the Kent Coast Electrification in June 1961, and this saw them off the Eastern Section; they went to the Western Section and were further strengthened as 10-coach sets with the addition of Seconds 45, 103 and 104 for Set 80, and Seconds 1932,1933 and 1934 (all ex Loose) for Set 86.

4-sets 'N' 81-4/5/7/8/91-4 remained on London-Dover-Ramsgate-Margate services for a while longer, as full electric services did not start until June 1962, and some trains were diesel-hauled until then.  The workings from 13th June, 1960, showed that local trains such as the 12.42 pm Ashford to Tonbridge and 4.12 pm Tonbridge to Margate were formed of a 4-set 'N'.  One 'business' train, the 6.21 pm from Cannon Street, had a 7-set 80 or 86 leading, and 4-set 'N' at the rear:  the train was divided at Tonbridge; the leading set ran to Ramsgate at 7.7 pm and the 4-set, after having two vans off the 5.25 pm London Bridge to Tunbridge Wells West (via Redhill and Tonbridge) added to the rear, left at 7.13 pm for Margate.

By September, 1961, some of the 4-sets were appearing regularly on the Tonbridge-Redhill-Reading lines, mostly on through trains to and from the Eastern Section, and usually diesel-hauled as far as Redhill.  Trains worked

by 4-sets were:

> 10.40 am Ashford to Redhill and Reading; 2.50 pm Reading to Redhill; 5.8 pm Redhill to Tonbridge.
> 2.41 pm Margate to Cannon Street, via Redhill.
> 4.58 pm Dover Priory to Redhill and Reading; returning next day on 6.5 am Reading to Margate.
> 4.50 am London Bridge to Margate, via Redhill.

From June 1962, all the 4-sets were on the Central Section, in particular providing passengers on the Horsham-Guildford and Horsham-Brighton lines with unaccustomed luxury for a short time. They also appeared on Tunbridge Wells-Eastbourne services. All were reduced to 3-sets by removing the corridor 2nd in each set in 1963, and continued work on the few remaining steam-hauled services on the Central Division: Tunbridge Wells-Eastbourne, Reading-Redhill-Tonbridge, and Horsham-Guildford.

First sets to be withdrawn were 81, 84, and 89 in May 1964, and 93 in June. From 15th June, 1964, they took over the workings of peak hour trains on Three Bridges-East Grinstead-Tunbridge Wells Services, which formerly had been the preserve of push and pull trains (diesel units having operated in the middle of the day since 1963). From 14th June, 1965, it was all over for steam operation on the Central: sets 87, 91 and 92 had been withdrawn earlier in the year, and the remainder, 82, 83, 85, 86 (a 3-set since June 1964), 88, 90, and 94, were transferred to the Western Section for West of England and Weymouth services. One further alteration had been made: in January 1965, Bke 2nd 4023 (set 86) was withdrawn and replaced by 3956 ex Set 266.

Although Set 86 was reduced to three coaches, Set 80 remained a 'long' set right up to 1965/6. In summer 1964, it was allocated to a Bournemouth-Sheffield working, alternating with 9-set 474 (described in the previous section). Official formation was 4011, 101, 103, 5823, 5785, 26, 102, 112, 4012.

Second brakes 4035/6 (set 92) were sold to the Chipman Company, Horsham, for use in its weedkilling trains which were painted red and white. 4035/6 were renumbered CWT 10 and CWT 12. CWT 10 later appeared in the new Chipman livery of pea green with white lettering.

## 'TAVERN' CARS AND RESTAURANT CARS, 1949

Whether one regards Mr. Bulleid's famous 'Tavern' cars as a success or a disaster depends on one's point of view either as a restaurateur or a diner. The Hotels Executive of the British Transport Commission certainly approved of the Tavern cars as they had a higher turnover than any another restaurant car on the Southern; but so vociferous were the howls of protest about the seating arrangement, and inability to view the passing scenery

while dining, that the restaurant cars were very quickly altered to a more conventional style.

The 'Tavern' car had a kitchen and pantry with a buffet section designed in the style of an old English tavern, and this car was intended to run with a first- and third-class dining saloon, the third-class end being coupled next to the kitchen end of the Tavern car.

The restaurant cars were numbered 7833 to 7840, and were built at Eastleigh in April (7833-5), May (7836-9) and June 1949 (7840). The kitchen cars were Nos. 7892-7899, built at the same time - the first three in April, four in May, and the last in June 1949. Body panels of both types were extended over solebars, like the Bournemouth dining sets.

Although Bulleid was given a free hand in carriage design, the Railway Executive insisted that all carriages must appear in the new standard livery, crimson lake and cream. Most remarkably, this livery was eminently suitable for application to Tavern cars! Externally, half of the car was painted in the orthodox livery, but the 'Tavern' part of the car had the lower crimson area lined out to represent a very good English Bond brickwork, and the upper cream portion had black stripes painted on to represent timber and plaster. An 'inn' sign, on a vitreous enamel plate about 2 ft 7 in. by 3 ft 4 in., was set on the outside of the car; each sign was specially painted for the coaches. No. 7892 was 'White Horse', 7893 'Jolly Tar', 7894 'Dolphin', 7895 'Bull', 7896 'Salutation', 7897 'Three Plovers', 7898 'Green Man', and 7899 'George & Dragon' (a contemporary source notes this one as being 'Crown', but probably the change was made before the car entered service). All these names were clumsily prefixed by the words 'At the Sign of the . . . '

There were a few official murmurings at this free interpretation of the standard coach livery, but when the first vehicles were inspected by Railway Executive Members, apparently nobody liked to say anything at the time.

Inside each Tavern car were dark oak settles seating 12, placed against the walls, and three 'refectory-type' tables. This section had small windows each side, set high in the body, with imitation small leaded panes. Old-type square metal lanterns hung from the ceiling beams, which were dark oak set into a rough-white ceiling. This ceiling was angled at the sides and horizontal in the centre to allow for the curvature of the roof. Even the floor covering was fake; it imitated the black-and-red tiling of a country pub. Unfortunately, the carefully-planned spuriousness gave out when the bar was reached; this was described as being a modern cocktail bar and snack counter of stainless steel and plastic! A small reproduction of the 'inn' sign was to be found here, hanging from one of the roof beams. Leaded swing doors led from the buffet section to the corridor, which passed the pantry, kitchen and staff compartment at the far end. The kitchen and pantry were finished in cream and chromium plate, with a special non-slip cream tiled

floor, and cream plastic-panelled walls. Thermostatically-controlled pressure ventilation was used in this car. Water tanks, oil-gas containers, and electrical apparatus for lighting, ventilation and refrigeration were all carried on the underframes below floor level; water was raised to kitchen sink level by air pressure. In later years, all cars were fitted for propane gas.

The Composite Restaurant Car had 24 first-class and 40 third-class seats, and one lavatory at the first-class end of the coach. First-class seats were ranged along each side, facing inwards, 12 on one side and 12 on the other. There were six tables each side of the central walkway, with just enough space between the tables for a passenger to squeeze past to get to his seat (two seats for each table). From the point of view of the stewards, this was an excellent arrangement: each meal could be placed on the table easily without having to stretch across, as with the normal transverse seating. Transverse seating was, however employed in the third-class part of the car: ten tables with four chairs at each table. Interior of this car was also 'half-timbered', but the use of polished light-oak for the timbers and wall frame, and buff plastic panels, gave a more modern effect. 'Concealed' fluorescent lighting was used; the only natural lighting was by standard 15 in. sliding ventilators, and the area below, where normally one would expect a large fixed pane of glass, was blank. This was a very unpleasing feature, but in defence of it the Southern stated that it was to preserve the 'antique' interior appearance, and that allowing passengers to view the scenery while dining might distract them and cause them to dally over their meals or refreshments.

The first two Tavern sets were placed on the 10.35 am Waterloo to Exeter service and the 12.50 pm Exeter to Waterloo (one journey each way daily). The others were initially allocated to the Eastern Region; but it is believed that all were on the Southern for the start of the winter services on 26th September, 1949, allocated to Waterloo-Exeter workings.

The complaints got results, and one by one the restaurant cars were modified, starting with No. 7836 in June 1950. Each car was given full-size windows, and new seating provided to the normal transverse arrangement. The first-class saloon, formerly 25 ft 3 1/4 in. long, was extended to 34 ft 8 in. and became the new third-class area, with six tables each side: tables on one side had four chairs each, and those on the other side of the walkway had two chairs each - total, 36. The now-reduced former third-class saloon became the first-class, with 18 seats: there were three tables for four on one side, and three tables for two on the other side of the walkway.

Other cars were reconstructed as follows: 7837 (7/50), 7838 (9/50), 7833 (10/50), 7840 (11/50), 7839 (2/51), 7835 (4/51), and 7834 (6/51). The Tavern cars were not altered at that time, although it is believed that the 'brickwork' was painted out; ultimately these, and the dining cars, were painted green, and the names were deleted from official lists from November, 1959.

Most of the Tavern sets worked between Waterloo and Exeter Central for the greater part of their time. The method of working at Exeter would be for a Down train to arrive, the front portion to be detached and continue on its way; a spare engine would then back down and remove the restaurant car set and any other cars that were to be detached; finally the rear portion of the train could then leave for the West. The Tavern set would be berthed on one of the central roads to be attached on to an Up train; the front portion on arriving would go right up to the London end of the platform and the Tavern set would then be backed on to it via the scissors crossover. Finally the rear portion would come in, halt clear of the scissors so that its locomotive could traverse it; then the front portion could set back a little and couple to the rear coaches.

Starting in 1959, the Taverns were altered to ordinary buffet cars. The bar counter was redesigned, the oak settles removed and replaced by two tables on one side (one with four chairs, the other with three) and four inward-facing seats and two tables on the other side. Two emergency external doors were included, as well as decent-sized windows. The kitchen and pantry areas were unaltered. All eight cars had been modified by June 1960, to Order No. 4339 (issued in September 1956).

Workings of the rebuilt Kitchen Buffet cars, and the open Composite trailers, from 12th September, 1960, were as shown below.

| Wkg. No | Car | Saloon | |
|---|---|---|---|
| 1 | 7899 | 7834 | 11.0 am W'loo-Exeter and 4.30 pm return. |
| 2 | 7894 | 7833 | 6.30 am Exeter-W'loo and 1.0 pm return. |
| 3 | 7892 | 7838 | Spare. |
| 4 | 7893 | 7836 | Spare. |
| 5 | 7895 | 7839 | 10.30 am Exeter-W'loo and 6.0 pm return. |
| 6 | 7897 | 7837 | 10.8 am B'mouth W.-W'loo and 6.30 pm return. |
| 7 | 7896 | 7835 | 12.30 pm Exeter-W'loo and 7.0 pm return. |
| 8 | 7898 | 7840 | 8.20 am B'mouth W.-W'loo and 4.35 pm return. ('ROYAL WESSEX') |

The cars allocated to Working No. 6 were normally formed in 6-set 805. The 'Royal Wessex' had started in June 1951 and was originally formed entirely of BR-built 1951 stock, including a kitchen-only car; but from June 1952 the Bulleid cars replaced the original restaurant vehicles, 7898 and 7840 being allocated to this train for many years.

First withdrawals were of Saloons 7833/4/7/40 in 1965; all were sold for scrap to Birds, Bynea, in April 1966. The other four saloons, and six of the buffet cars, lasted up to the end of steam working on the Bournemouth line, and were in regular use until then. No. 7894 was condemned in March 1967 but reinstated, condemned again in July 1967 and reprieved yet again, and finally condemned in January 1968.

## 'LOOSE' COACHES, 1949 TO 1950

We now come to a somewhat complicated part of the story. The coaches built from mid-1949 to early 1950 were intended as loose stock, but many of them did in fact enter traffic formed in sets; it is clear that this must have been a late decision, as the coaches formed in the sets did not go in numerical order, and were doubtless selected as convenient from the long lines of stock that stood about for some time following completion.

The first to appear in traffic, in September, 1949, was a batch of 40 corridor firsts, Nos. 7608 to 7647. Each one had seven compartments seating 42 passengers; layout comprised a transverse vestibule at one end, four compartments, transverse vestibule, three compartments, transverse vestibule, and two lavatory compartments divided by a short central corridor. Side corridor was on the right-hand side when viewed from the lavatory end of the coach. External livery was B.R. crimson lake and cream, and the number, with 'S' prefix, appeared on the waist at the left-hand end of the coach.

Building dates:  7608/9 - June 1949.  7610-20 - July 1949.  7621/2 - September 1949.  7623 - July 1949.  7624-37 - August 1949.  7638-47 - September 1949.  Built to Order No. 3450.

The next lot of loose coaches were twenty Third Brakes; but most of these were formed into sets for the Eastern Section in time for the start of summer train services in June, 1950.  Coach numbers were 3943 to 3957, built September 1949; and 3958 to 3962, built October 1949.  These Third Brakes were identical to the ones in sets 80 to 94, but were painted in crimson lake and cream with number on the waist at the left-hand end. Order No. 3451.

Next came a batch of forty Composites, Nos. 5868 to 5907, which were identical to those in sets 80 to 94.  Building dates: 5868-72 - October 1949; 5873-5900 - November 1949; and 5901-7 - December 1949. Order No. 3452. All were in traffic by June, 1950, several in sets on the Eastern Section, which could not be formed immediately until the Thirds (see below) were completed early in 1950.  However, it was found possible to make up three additional 3-sets 'L' from the stock already built, and the formation of these was:-

|           | Set 767 | Set 768 | Set 769 |
|-----------|---------|---------|---------|
| Thd.Bke   | 3950    | 3952    | 3954    |
| Compo.    | 5878    | 5880    | 5879    |
| Thd. Bke  | 3951    | 3953    | 3955    |

They were allocated from June 1950 to London-Dover-Ramsgate-Margate. services, remaining on these until June, 1955. Finally came 40 Thirds, Nos. 41 to 80. It is believed that all were originally intended to be formed in new 5-sets 830-849 (see next section) but Nos. 41 to 56 were 'diverted', and, instead of appearing in sets 830 to 837, were formed in 'long' sets for the

Eastern Section. Nos. 57 to 80 were placed as intended in 5-sets 838 to 849.

These corridor thirds, which were the same as those in sets 80-94, were built as follows: - 41-46 - January 1950; 47-62 - February 1950; and 63-80 - March 1950. Built to Order No. 3453, they weighed 33 tons each.

It is now convenient to give the formations of the four sets made up from examples of the foregoing stock: Sets Nos. 264 to 267, which were all used on London-Ramsgate services until June, 1959. Sets 265, 266 and 267 always included a Maunsell restaurant car in the formation; in 1954 these were rebuilt as buffet cars, but remained on the same workings.

| Set 264 | | Set 265 | | Set 266 | | Set 267 | |
|---|---|---|---|---|---|---|---|
| Thd. Bke. | 3946 | Thd. Bke. | 3959 | Thd. Bke. | 3956 | Thd. Bke. | 3948 |
| Third | 55 | Third | 41 | Third | 46 | Third | 43 |
| Compo. | 5881 | Compo. | 5868 | Third | 47 | Third | 44 |
| Compo. | 5882 | Compo. | 5869 | Compo. | 5875 | Compo. | 5871 |
| Third | 56 | Compo. | 5870 | Compo. | 5876 | Compo. | 5872 |
| Thd. Bke. | 3947 | Res.Car | - | Res. Car | - | Compo. | 5873 |
| | | Third | 42 | Third | 48 | Compo. | 5874 |
| | | Thd. Bke. | 3960 | Third | 49 | Res. Car | - |
| | | | | Third | 50 | Third | 45 |
| | | | | Thd. Bke. | 3957 | Thd. Bke | 3949 |

Additionally, Composites 5883, 5884 and 5885 were placed in a 'Special Traffic' set, No. 263 - rather a waste of brand-new coaches, as such sets made only a few trips each year, and spent most of their time standing in sidings. This particular one must have looked rather odd, as it included Maunsell 9 ft wide corridor thirds 818, 819, 1176 and 1177, and 8 ft 6 in. - wide 'Continental' Third Brakes 3552 and 3558. By June 1955, the three Bulleid Compos had been removed, and were transferred to loose stock; during this period, from June 1950 to June 1955, the set had been stabled at Stewarts Lane during the currency of the summer timetables (June-September), and at Eardley at other times.

Alterations to the sets were made over the years: 264 - unchanged until September 1958, when Maunsell Corridor Seconds 1847 and 1864 were added. 1864 removed, 6/1959, and set transferred to a London-Dover-Margate service. Second 1847 to Loose, 2/1961; Bulleid Seconds 81 and 82 added, and set transferred to South Western Division. Reduced to 3-set, with 3946, 5881, and 3947, in June 1963 and transferred to Central Division for Three Bridges-Tunbridge Wells-Eastbourne, Horsham-Guildford, and Reading-Tonbridge services. Finally, to South Western Division in June 1965 as 3-set until condemnation in December, 1965.

Set 265: Buffet Car placed between 5868 and 5869 from June 1954. Compo 5907, ex Loose, added in June 1955. Set disbanded in June 1959, all stock going to Loose except 5868/9, which were placed in Set 263 for a short

The Compartment side of 59 ft Corridor Third Brake No. 2876; the date painted on the solebar is '6/2/46'. *Eastleigh Carriage Works*

The Corridor side of Corridor Composite No. 5726, for Set 980, dated '4/4/46'.

Eastleigh Carriage Works

The Bournemouth 6-Dining Set 290 (August 1947) posed probably at Wallers Ash; this set, alone of the 290-300 series, had coaches with black ends. *Eastleigh Carriage Works*

The prototype Corridor Composite of 1945, No. 5751. Note the class numerals on the doors and the lack of ventilators in the frosted-glass lights. *Eastleigh Carriage Works*

The coaches forming 6-Dining Set No. 300, dated on the solebars '1/3/48' are shown in the next pages and are from Official photographs taken at Eastleigh Carriage Works. Open Third 1461.

Corridor Third Brake (semi-open) 4369.

*Eastleigh Carriage Works*

Corridor Composite 5750.

Eastleigh Carriage Works

Corridor Dining First No. 7687. Note the headboards.

Eastleigh Carriage Works

Kitchen/Dining Third No. 7891. Both this and the previous carriage were for Set 300, dated '1/3/48'; with green ends.

*Eastleigh Carriage Works*

time, finally going to Loose later in 1959.

Set 266: Unchanged until June 1959; buffet car removed, and set berthed at Margate for special traffic. To South Western Division, June 1961, and Corridor Second 50 removed and to Loose stock. To Central Division June 1963 for same duties as Set 264, reduced to 3-set with 3956, 5875, and 3957. 5875 was condemned in November 1964; 3956 to set 86 and 3957 to set 861.

Set 267: Buffet Car placed between 5872 and 5873 from June 1956. No other changes; set disbanded in June 1959, all coaches becoming loose stock.

After formation into sets in 1950 of the various batches, the balance retained as loose stock comprised Thirds 51 to 54, Third Brakes 3943-5/58/61/2, and Composites 5877/86-5907. Some of the Firsts were formed in Ocean Liner Boat Train sets 350 to 354 from June 1951, but details of these will be found in the section on '1950/1 Open Thirds'. Photographic evidence indicates that the Loose Third Brakes were used exclusively on Folkestone and Dover Boat Trains, one being formed at the 'country' end of each train, very conspicuous in its crimson and cream livery where all other coaches were green.

Over the years, much of the loose stock was gathered up into sets. In particular, three of the BR standard 4-car sets, Nos. 874, 875 and 876, introduced in 1952, were permanently strengthened from June 1953 by the addition of Bulleid stock - probably on the thinking that, as all three sets were operated on regular workings, it was more convenient to have the extra coaches as part of the sets instead of outside them. Sets 874 and 875 were used on regular London-Ramsgate services, and 876 on Oxted Line business trains. Formations:

| Set 874 | | Set 875 | | Set 876 | |
|---------|---------|---------|---------|---------|---------|
| Thd. Bke. | 34249 (BR) | Thd. Bke. | 34251 (BR) | Thd. Bke. | 34253 (BR) |
| Third | 24310 (BR) | Third | 24311 (BR) | Third | 24312 (BR) |
| Third | 51 (SR) | Third | 84 (SR) | First | 7631 (SR) |
| Compo. | 15032 (BR) | Compo. | 15033 (BR) | Compo | 15034 (BR) |
| Compo. | 5903 (SR) | Compo. | 5899 (SR) | Third | 54 (SR) |
| Third | 52 (SR) | Third | 88 (SR) | Thd. Bke. | 34254 (BR) |
| Third | 53 (SR) | Third | 89 (SR) | | |
| Thd. Bke. | 34250 (BR) | Thd. Bke. | 34252 (BR) | | |

In June, 1955, a further BR 4-set, 873, was increased to 8 cars, using two other BR vehicles and Bulleid Composite 5892 and Third 91, and this also worked between London and Ramsgate. Bulleid and BR vehicles were ill-matched: the profile differed, the Standard bodyside curve being gentler than the SR one; and the smooth steel roofs of the BR coaches rather showed-up the coarse texture of the canvas covering the SR stock. The contrast was made even more pointed around 1958, as the Bulleid coaches in all four sets were repainted green but the BR coaches were left in their crimson and cream

for a few years more; the sets looked very untidy, as though someone had sprinkled a few green coaches entirely at random into each train. With a 1954-converted Maunsell buffet car in the middle, and the whole ensemble hauled in the last months by an unkempt Class 'N' 2-6-0 instead of a gleaming 'Battle of Britain' 4-6-2, some of the spirit of the South Eastern and Chatham was captured.

From June 1959, set 873 was a special Traffic set berthed at Grove Park; and Nos. 874 and 875 were also for special traffic, stabled at Grove Park or Deal. From June 1960, all three were on London-Dover-Margate workings; in 1961 873 went to the Central Section and the other two to the Western. No. 876 stayed on the Oxted Line until 1962, being used on the favourite 4.40 pm London Bridge to Brighton. By 1963, all the Bulleid vehicles had been removed from the four sets.

From June, 1955, 3-sets 'L' Nos. 767 to 769 were transferred from the Dover line to the Oxted Line, and No. 767 was made up to eight coaches for regular workings between London and Tunbridge Wells West. The extra coaches were First 7645, and Thirds 93, 94, 95 and 96 - which were formed outside the Third Brakes, two at each end of the train. No. 767 was in fact a direct replacement of Maunsell set 194, which had had a similar composition since 1947. Most platforms on the Oxted Line were only long enough for six coaches, and this arrangement ensured that the guard would always be alongside the platform at stops. Nevertheless, from June 1959, 767 was re-formed with the Seconds inside the train, with the result that the guard now had to walk up the train for every stop. It was quite the most splendid train in regular use on this line, and was always on the 7.55 am Groombridge to London Bridge and 5.49 pm Victoria to Groombridge. From June 1962 it was reduced to seven vehicles by removing Compo 5878; and altered to a 3-set formed 3950, 5889, 3951 by June 1964 and sent to the South Western Division.

3-sets 768 and 769 stayed on London-Forest Row-Tunbridge Wells workings until June 1959, when they went to the South Western for Waterloo-West of England and Waterloo-Weymouth services, being kept as 3-sets 'L' until June 1963.

In April 1957 two new sets, 803 and 804, were made up for working between London and East Grinstead; each comprised four Maunsell coaches and one Bulleid (Compos 5904 in 803 and 5883 in 804). Two years later, No. 804 was re-formed entirely with Bulleid vehicles, all ex Loose:- Second Brake 3944, Compo 5883, Seconds 1935 and 1936, Second Brake 3945. No. 803 was similarly altered late in 1961, with Second Brakes 3948 and 3960, and Seconds 88 and 89. In 1962, set 803 had an additional First, 7634, and began working on the 7.27 am Reading to London Bridge and 5.25 pm return.

By June 1964, both had been made up to 10-sets: No. 803 for Brighton-Bournemouth (S.X.) and Eastbourne-Walsall service (S.O.); and No. 804 for

Eastbourne-Wolverhampton services. Formation was now:-

| 803 | 2nd Bke. | 3948 | | 804 | 2nd Bke. | 3944 | |
|-----|----------|------|---------|-----|----------|------|---------|
| | Second | 122 | Ex 802 | | Second | 45 | Ex 80 |
| | Second | 97 | Ex 801 | | Second | 1935 | |
| | Second | 33 | Ex 87 | | Second | 88 | Ex 803 |
| | Compo. | 5904 | | | Compo. | 5883 | |
| | Compo. | 5888 | Ex Loose | | Compo. | 5894 | Ex 432 |
| | Second | 37 | Ex 91 | | Second | 1936 | |
| | Second | 29 | Ex 83 | | Second | 54 | Ex 876 |
| | Second | 30 | Ex 84 | | Second | 89 | Ex 803 |
| | 2nd Bke. | 3960 | | | 2nd Bke. | 3945 | |

The following summer, No. 803 was used on an Eastbourne-Wolverhampton service, and 804, with a further Second added (50, ex 807 set), was on the Margate-Wolverhampton service.

In March, 1958, a further set for the Oxted Line, No. 897, was formed, using Second Brakes 4225 and 4226 of 1948, three Maunsell Seconds and a First. Late in 1959, Bulleid Seconds 41, 42 and 43 were substituted, spare since the abolition of Kent Coast sets 265 and 267; and in December the Maunsell First was replaced by Bulleid First 7646, Ex Loose. 6-set 897 ran on regular workings between Tunbridge Wells West and London.

That completes the survey of the more important sets and reformations made from the original 'loose' coaches of 1949/50; the only other point that should be made is that all were ultimately repainted in BR green livery, by about 1960; and that loose Composite 5898 was withdrawn in April 1953 (the shortest-lived Bulleid coach) following - presumably - a shunting accident.

### SETS 830 TO 849, 1950

Eight of these sets first entered traffic as three-coach, but the remaining twelve were five-coach from the start; during each summer season, the 3-coach sets were strengthened to 5-coach by the addition of two corridor thirds each, which were removed at the start of the winter timetable every year; and ultimately all became permanent 5-coach sets.

That briefly summarises the extraordinarily complex history of these particular sets, which were always allocated to the Western Section, and which were introduced in time for the start of the summer train services in June, 1950.

The coaches themselves were perfectly standard, with large window ventilators and short stepboards; and were painted in crimson lake and cream livery with number (prefixed 'S') on the waist at the left-hand of the vehicle.

Third Brakes and Composites were built in reverse numerical order (not normal Eastleigh practice, and the reason why may be known only by those

who were there at the time). Building dates were:

Third Brakes: 4006-10 - February 1950. 4001-5 - March 1950. 3982-4000 - April 1950. 3974-81 - May 1950. 3971-3 - July 1950. Order No. 3454.

Composites: 5858-67 - March 1950. 5848-57 - May 1950. Order No. 3454.

Sets 830 to 837 were 3-coach originally, formed with Third Brakes 3971 to 3986 and Compos 5848 to 5855, all in numerical order. Sets 838 to 849 were always 5-coach, and incorporated Thirds Nos. 57 to 80, built in February and March 1950 (part of Order No. 3453). It has been stated elsewhere[1] that Thirds Nos. 41 to 56 were in sets 830 to 837, but this is not so, although it may have been the original intention. Instead, these particular Thirds were formed in Eastern Section sets, as detailed in the previous section.

Sets 838 to 849 had Third Brakes 3987 to 4010 and Thirds 57 to 80 (all in numerical pairs and in order), and Composites 5856 to 5867. The formation of each 5-set was supposed to be: Third Brake, Third, Compo., Third, Third Brake: this applied also to the 'seasonal' 5-sets, but it sometimes happened that the two Thirds would be formed between the Compo and one Third Brake, this being easier and quicker for the shunters.

The large batch of loose Corridor Thirds, which had started with No. 41, was continued from No. 81 and completed with No. 130. Nos. 81 to 90 were completed in July 1950; 91 to 94 in August; 95 to 111 in September; and 112 to 130 in October 1950. These were built to Order No. 3580, and had long water tanks. It was this 'float' of vehicles which was drawn on for the annual summer strengthening: from June to September, 1951, for example, Sets 833 to 837 included Nos. 112, 105 (833); 102, 109 (834); 113, 122 (835); 100, 125 (836); and 120, 106 (837). In the following summer, Nos. 830 to 837 were all strengthened; but from June, 1953, Nos. 834 to 837 became permanent 5-sets, incorporating Thirds 123 to 130 in order and in numerical pairs. From then on, only Sets 830 to 833 were seasonal 5-sets, reverting to 3-car for the winter services, until July 1959 when at last they too became permanent 5-sets, with Seconds 114 to 121 formed in numerical order.

The sets in which most of the remaining loose thirds were placed have already been described; by June 1957 Nos. 81 to 98 and 122 were all formed permanently in sets, leaving only Nos. 99 to 121 as loose stock. In July 1959 Nos. 106 to 113 were placed in Birmingham R.C. & W. 3-sets Nos. 826 to 829, making them up to permanent 5-sets.

From 1959 until May 1964 the position remained stable; no further alterations were made to sets 830 to 849, and the workings still included Waterloo-Salisbury-West of England and Waterloo-Bournemouth-Weymouth. Corridor Second 127 in set 836 was withdrawn in May 1964 and replaced by No. 81 ex set 264; Second 119 in set 832 was withdrawn in September 1964 and replaced by 82 ex loose stock (formerly in set 264); Compo 5856 in set 838 was withdrawn in February 1965, being replaced by

former loose Composite No. 5807. No further alterations were made until the abolition of set train working round about the end of 1965.

## LOOSE OPEN THIRDS, 1950/1

These Open Thirds had the same internal layout as those in the Bournemouth dining sets, but the external appearance was the same as all the later Bulleid coaches. They appeared in crimson lake and cream livery, but with the car number on the waist on the right-hand side, this position having by late 1950 been settled as standard; the only likely reason for this seemingly piffling change is that the number in its new position could more easily be seen in conjunction with the dimension, tare and route restriction plates which were always fixed at the bottom left-hand side of the coach end. Coaches had LMS design switchboxes and long water tanks.

There were 45 Open Thirds, Nos. 1462 to 1506, and they were completed in November 1950 (1462-77), December 1950 (1478-1500) and January 1951 (1501-6). Order No. 3581. All were in traffic by June, 1951, many of them being formed in five new sets, Nos. 350 to 354, which were allocated exclusively to Waterloo-Southampton Docks Ocean Liner Boat Trains. These sets were originally formed thus:-

|  | 350 | 351 | 352 |  |  | 353 | 354 |
|---|---|---|---|---|---|---|---|
| Compo Bke. | 6649* | 6662* | 6650* | Compo Bke. |  | 6570* | 6644* |
| Open Third | 1476 | 1467 | 1469 | Open Third |  | 1496 | 1463 |
| Open Third | 1477 | 1502 | 1501 | Open Third |  | 1486 | 1472 |
| Cor. First | 7610 | 7627 | 7609 | Open Third |  | 1499 | 1503 |
| Open Third | 1478 | 1468 | 1498 | Open Third |  | 1481 | 1504 |
| Open Third | 1479 | 1495 | 1485 | Cor. First |  | 7608 | 7621 |
| Open Third | 1480 | 1475 | 1491 | Cor. First |  | 7618 | 7620 |
| Compo Bke. | 6601* | 6587* | 6669* | Compo. Bke |  | 6651* | 7711† |

* Maunsell cor. brake composite.          † 'Ironclad' cor. brake first.

Alterations to sets: 350 - 1476-80, 7610 to loose, replaced by 1505, 1462, 7617, 1482, 1500, 1470, June 1953. 352 - 7609 to set 353, replaced by 7619 ex loose, June 1952. 353 - 7608 to loose, replaced by 7609 ex-set 352, June 1952. Finally in 1954, all the Bulleid Open Thirds were replaced by new BR standard open thirds, and the Bulleid vehicles went to the loose stock list, being reserved mainly for 'special formation' boat trains. Then in 1959 Nos. 1477/9 were formed in set 80, and 1482/7 in set 86, both of which were in use on the Eastern Section until 1961, and on the Western until 1962.

In 1964, two Special Traffic sets, No. 212 for the Central Division, and 770 for the South Western, were made up using many of the 1950 open seconds. No. 212 was in fact a long-standing special traffic set, first appearing in 1953

composed of Maunsell vehicles; but by June 1964 all the coaches were Bulleids except one BR open first. Set 770 utilised the Second Brakes of the former 3-set 'L' 770, but was otherwise new. Formations: 212-4353 (ex set 292), 1500, 1504, 1468, 3514 open first, 1476, 1457, 1453, 1456, 4354 (ex292). 770 - 4301, 1496, 1501, 1491, 3504 open first, 1503, 1486, 1452 (ex 291), 1465, 4302. Second brakes 4353/4 were replaced by 4349/50 ex set 290 by June 1965; and 1463 replaced open first 3504 in set 770, which then became second-class only and was extensively used on those tortuously-routed railtours so beloved of enthusiasts at that period.

## SETS 850 TO 865, 1951

These were the last sets of Bulleid stock to enter traffic, although loose corridor first No. 7648 was actually the very last coach. Sets 850 to 857, for London-Dover-Ramsgate-Margate services, were three-coach; but Nos. 858 to 865, introduced in time for the summer 1951 train services, went into service as 5-coach sets for the Waterloo-Salisbury-West of England lines. In each case, the extra coaches comprised two unspecified corridor thirds.

Sets 850 to 865 were each formed of two Third Brakes and one Composite, similar in appearance to those in sets 830 to 849; the underframes, however, were equipped with LMS design switch control boxes and the water tanks were longer. The Composites, Nos. 5908 to 5923, were built well before they were required, construction following on immediately after the 5868-5907 batch: 5908 was completed in December 1949, 5909-5918 in January 1950 and 5919-5923 in February. The Third Brakes, Nos. 2501 to 2532, were completed much later: Nos. 2501-8 in February 1951; 2509-14 in March; 2515-22 in April; 2523-5/7 in May; and 2526/8-32 in June 1951. Third Brakes weighed 33 tons each and Composites 34 tons. All coaches built to Order No. 3583. The sets were assembled with all coaches in numerical order. Livery was crimson lake and cream, with numbers on the waist in the right-hand position.

Sets 858 to 865 were reduced to three coaches from 10 September, 1951, but increased again to 5-car for the summer 1952 services. The extra corridor thirds were specified as 107, 130 (858); 105, 129 (859); 114, 116 (860); 102, 101(862); 121, 117 (863). The following September only sets 862-865 reverted to three-coach; but by June, 1953, all were now 3-sets and remained so.

Sets 850 to 857 continued working on the Eastern Section until June, 1955, when Nos. 851-7 were transferred to the Western, and 850 alone went to the Oxted Line and worked in the same diagrams as 1949-built 3-sets 768 and 769. From June 1959 this set also left to join its sisters on the Western Section; and so the whole series was now in the same operating area.

About 1960 the intermediate buffers were removed from the coaches in

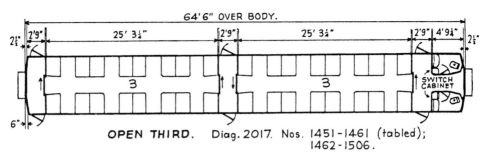

**OPEN THIRD.** Diag. 2017. Nos. 1451-1461 (tabled); 1462-1506.

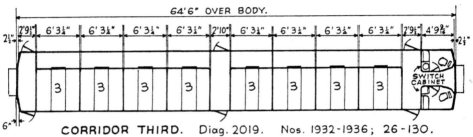

**CORRIDOR THIRD.** Diag. 2019. Nos. 1932-1936; 26-130.

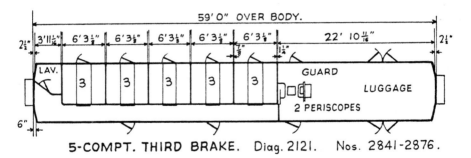

**5-COMPT. THIRD BRAKE.** Diag. 2121. Nos. 2841-2876.

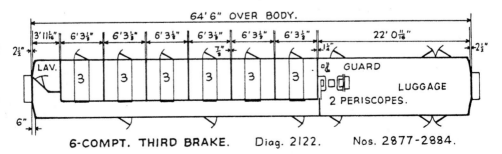

**6-COMPT. THIRD BRAKE.** Diag. 2122. Nos. 2877-2884.

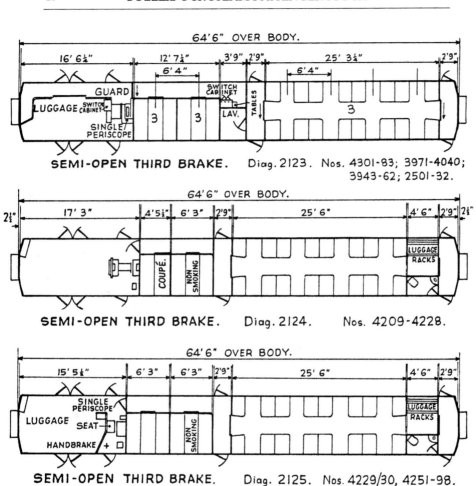

**SEMI-OPEN THIRD BRAKE.**  Diag. 2123.  Nos. 4301-83; 3971-4040; 3943-62; 2501-32.

**SEMI-OPEN THIRD BRAKE.**  Diag. 2124.  Nos. 4209-4228.

**SEMI-OPEN THIRD BRAKE.**  Diag. 2125.  Nos. 4229/30, 4251-98.

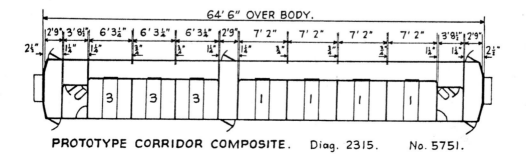

**PROTOTYPE CORRIDOR COMPOSITE.**  Diag. 2315.  No. 5751.

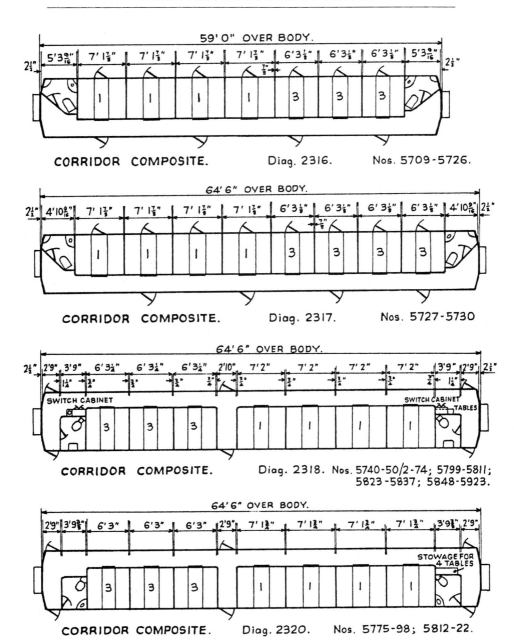

CORRIDOR COMPOSITE.    Diag. 2316.    Nos. 5709-5726.

CORRIDOR COMPOSITE.    Diag. 2317.    Nos. 5727-5730

CORRIDOR COMPOSITE.    Diag. 2318. Nos. 5740-50/2-74; 5799-5811; 5823-5837; 5848-5923.

CORRIDOR COMPOSITE.    Diag. 2320.    Nos. 5775-98; 5812-22.

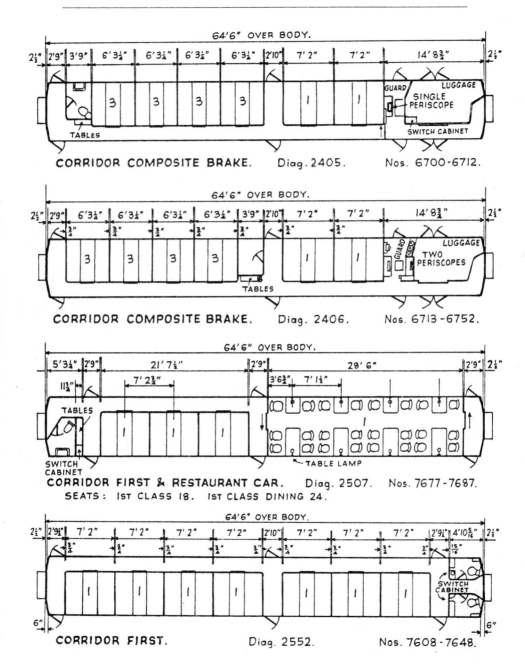

**CORRIDOR COMPOSITE BRAKE.**    Diag. 2405.     Nos. 6700-6712.

**CORRIDOR COMPOSITE BRAKE.**    Diag. 2406.     Nos. 6713-6752.

**CORRIDOR FIRST & RESTAURANT CAR.**    Diag. 2507.    Nos. 7677-7687.
SEATS: 1st CLASS 18.    1st CLASS DINING 24.

**CORRIDOR FIRST.**      Diag. 2552.     Nos. 7608-7648.

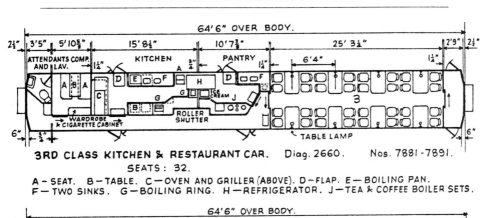

**3RD CLASS KITCHEN & RESTAURANT CAR.** Diag. 2660. Nos. 7881-7891.

SEATS : 32.

A - SEAT. B - TABLE. C - OVEN AND GRILLER (ABOVE). D - FLAP. E - BOILING PAN.
F - TWO SINKS. G - BOILING RING. H - REFRIGERATOR. J - TEA & COFFEE BOILER SETS.

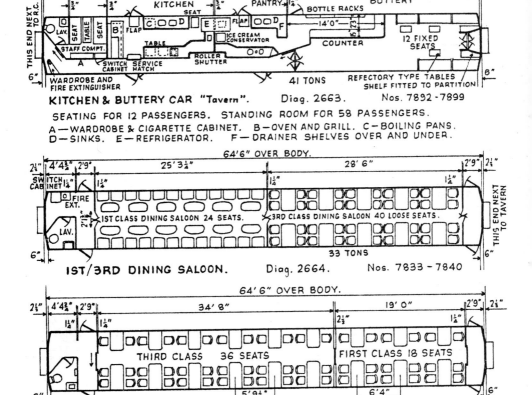

**KITCHEN & BUTTERY CAR "Tavern".** Diag. 2663. Nos. 7892-7899

SEATING FOR 12 PASSENGERS. STANDING ROOM FOR 58 PASSENGERS.
A - WARDROBE & CIGARETTE CABINET. B - OVEN AND GRILL. C - BOILING PANS.
D - SINKS. E - REFRIGERATOR. F - DRAINER SHELVES OVER AND UNDER.

**1ST/3RD DINING SALOON.** Diag. 2664. Nos. 7833-7840

**COMPOSITE SALOON.** Diag. 2665. Nos. 7833-7840.
Rebuilt from Diag. 2664.

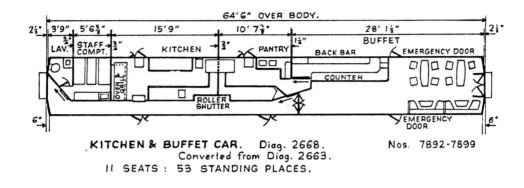

**KITCHEN & BUFFET CAR.** Diag. 2668.          Nos. 7892-7899
Converted from Diag. 2663.
II SEATS : 53 STANDING PLACES.

**INSPECTION SALOON**     Diag. 1873          No. 100 s.

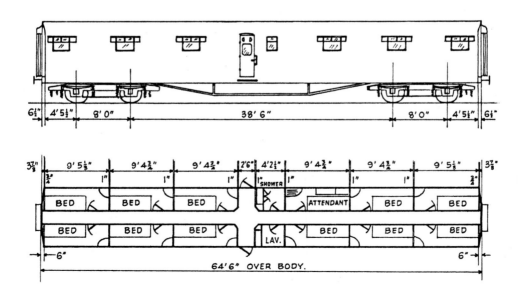

sets 850 to 865; although side buffers were never used normally, it could have been awkward if a coach had found itself next to a non automatic buckeye-coupled vehicle - but these sets did in fact stay intact, and by 1964 the intermediate buffers had been restored as withdrawals started. In 1962, set 864 was reduced to 2 coaches (2530, 5922) for working the Swanage portion of the 'Royal Wessex'.

The first set to be withdrawn from service was 856, in April 1964. Set 864 was disbanded in 1963, 2530 going to loose stock, and 5922 going to set 858. 5916, also in set 858, became loose in 1964. 2532 (set 865) was withdrawn in April 1964, being replaced by 4352 ex set 291. 2523 (set 861) was withdrawn 1/1965 and replaced by 3957 ex set 266. Other sets withdrawn intact before the dissolution of those remaining in early 1966 were: 851 (Dec. 1965), 860 (Nov. 1965) and 865 (Dec. 1965).

During 1964, Nos. 854 and 855 ran as 6-sets and were used on the Ramsgate-Wolverhampton service; the extra coaches were Maunsell corridor seconds: 1211, 1824 and 1887 in set 854, and 1265, 1277 and 1879 in set 855. Between 1962 and 1965, No. 858 also ran with extra coaches, which were periodically switched about; this set was allocated to a Waterloo-Weymouth service.

### CORRIDOR FIRST No. 7648 (Order No. 3582)

This solitary coach, the last Bulleid-style corridor vehicle, was completed in July 1951 and was the same as the 1949-built Firsts 7608-7647. Why the Southern decided it just had to have one more First is another of those mysteries; it entered service as a loose vehicle, ran in set 473 from 1954 to 1959, and to set 299 in 1965. Again loose from 1966 until its withdrawal in December 1967.

### BULLEID COACHES FROM 1966 TO 1968

From about March, 1966, the use of properly-formed set trains, with painted set numbers, was abandoned by the Southern Region. Up to then, during the previous three or four years, several of the sets had suffered many changes in make-up owing to withdrawals of individual coaches, and there were also far more cases than previously noted of sets running with temporary coaches and not conforming to the official formations as laid down in the Appendices to Carriage Working Notices. Probably most of the 'long' sets had been disbanded before March, 1966, from about September, 1965; but many of the 3-coach sets were still intact at this time: Mr. M.S. King noted the coaches of set 788 in April, 1966, still together and with the set numbers at each end freshly painted over, the figures being discernible

under the black patch of paint. By July, only two of the coaches were still running together.

It may have been felt that with withdrawals taking place so rapidly, operation of set trains had become meaningless. Work on electrifying the Bournemouth line was now in progress, and Bulleid coaches were scheduled for mass withdrawal when this was completed. In other words, there was no interest in them; they were being run down and it didn't matter how messy and untidy the trains looked, as that would make the replacing electric stock look all the smarter. The steam trains certainly did look 'untidy', with examples of the four main designs often to be found in one train; possibly a few BR coaches sprinkled in (these were starting to be repainted in blue and grey - a livery never applied to any Bulleid steam-hauled coach on the Southern); and, aesthetically most displeasing of all, a brake coach marshalled the 'wrong way round'.

The Appendix to Carriage Working Notices dated 13th June, 1966, showed that sets of a sort were in use: formations and number of seats were shown, but no vehicle numbers. As a result it mattered not at all whether the Composites, Corridor Seconds or Open Seconds used were Bulleid or BR vehicles, as both versions of each type had the same seating capacity. The following, however, were booked to include 48-seat (Bulleid) Corridor Brake Seconds as opposed to the BR (32-seat) version:

One 11-set (Margate-Wolverhampton); one 10-set (special traffic, Central Division); one 10-set (Eastbourne-Wolverhampton); one 7-buffet set (Victoria-Newhaven Harbour); two 8 Kitchen Buffet sets (Waterloo-Exeter); two 6-Buffet sets (Waterloo-Bournemouth); one 6 Kitchen Buffet set (Waterloo-Bournemouth); one 9-set (Waterloo-Bournemouth-Swanage); four 8-sets (40-seat Second Brakes) (Waterloo-Bournemouth and Waterloo-Exeter); 43 3-sets (Waterloo-Weymouth-Portsmouth); and one 10-set (special traffic, South Western Division).

There were also two 4-Miniature Buffet sets for Waterloo-Salisbury-Exeter services, each with one Bulleid second brake and one compo brake; and five 2-sets for 'Bournemouth Local Working' (doubtless the Swanage and Lymington branches) formed of a Bulleid brake compo and corridor second.

The list of surviving Bulleid coaches as at June 1966 showed 108 corridor seconds, including the four downgraded composites 1727-30; 34 open seconds; 117 48-seat second brakes and nine 40-seaters; 83 corridor composites; 12 corridor brake composites; two corridor firsts (7616/48), 8 kitchen/buffet cars (7892-9), two restaurant first saloons (7677/83); and four restaurant composite saloons (7835/6/8/9). The list also showed 29 composites as downgraded to seconds (with 56 seats each) but it is not clear if these downgradings were actually carried out. It was intended that they should have been

altered from May 1966, but that none was to be renumbered into the second-class series. M.S. King, who travelled frequently on the Bournemouth and Salisbury lines in 1966, never saw any; he feels sure that if any downgraded first-class compartments had been available he would have found them! All retained their 'Compo' numbers.

The Appendix also gave advance information for March 1967 which included the theoretical formations of entirely new sets divided into three groups; Electric Heating - Air Brake; Dual Heating - Vacuum Brake; and Steam Heating - Vacuum Brake. The instruction was that, from 13th June, 1966, each coach going into works would have its new set number painted on - and that was precisely what happened; none of the new sets was actually formed until about mid-1967, and this had to be done with coaches that often were scattered at different ends of the system. Several of the theoretical sets never were correctly formed.

In most cases, this scheme applied only to BR stock; but in 1966, it was intended that some examples of Bulleid stock should survive the purge and be formed into four of the 1967 sets, all of which were to retain steam heating and vacuum brakes. Open Seconds 1504 and 1490 would go in 7-Kitchen Buffet set No. 180; 1481 to 8-Kitchen Buffet set 185; 1494 to 8-Kitchen Buffet set 186 (all Waterloo-Exeter sets); and 1506, 1488, 1493, 1475 and 1501 would go in 10-Miniature Buffet set 195 (Waterloo-Weymouth Quay). Additionally, Nos. 1460/3/5/83/5/ 92/6/7 were to be loose coaches. If these vehicles had been retained, they would have been repainted in blue and grey, but unfortunately this part of the scheme was not carried out. By the time sets 180, 185 and 186 started to be formed (late 1967) some BR open seconds had been acquired and were put in the sets instead. (Set 195 never was formed). Set 186 was also to include an S.R. kitchen/buffet car, but there was some uncertainty as to whether it should be ex-Tavern car 7899 or Maunsell car 7969; in the event, neither was used.

As with the Maunsell coaches a few years earlier, withdrawal of Bulleid stock took place faster than the coaches could be sent off to scrapyards, and sidings at Barnes, Hamworthy Junction, Richmond, Twickenham, and Walton-on-Thames (Oatlands) were filled with condemned vehicles awaiting disposal. The following vehicles were observed in sidings during 1966: 2501/2/7/8, Barnes 9/66; 2515, Micheldever 11/66; 2527/8, Oatlands 7/66; 2843, Micheldever, 11/66; 2851/75, 3950, Oatlands 5/66; 3953/71, 4007, Micheldever 1/66; 3988, Barnes 9/66; 4039/40, Eastleigh Yard 7/66; 4256/87, 4343/51/2/72, Barnes 9/66; 5787, Basingstoke 9/66; 5906, Andover 9/66.

The following were sold to Shipbreakers Queenborough for scrap: 3-sets 969, 971, 972 (3/64); 2523, 5/65; 3961, 9/64; 4293/4, 4/65; 5756, 5/65; 5791, 5/65; 5820, 4/65; 5835, 7/65, 5873 (the body of this was cut into halves, which were then placed at right-angles to each other on a patch of waste ground at

Queenborough - still there, 5/77); 5875, 5/65; 5878, 6/65; 6749, 9/64; 7613/80, about 6/65. Many others were sold to Bird's of Long Marston and King's of Wymondham.

What occurred to the 10.30 Waterloo to Weymouth train on 3rd September, 1966, must have been very disconcerting to the passengers. The rear coach of the train of Bulleid stock began to detach itself, and the train came to a stand near Wallers Ash. The bewildered passengers in this coach then had to climb down on to the ballast and walk along to board the rest of the train, which then continued its journey. The rear vehicle was removed by a locomotive run from Micheldever.

This incident was noted in *The Railway Magazine*; but a similar mishap had occurred in May that same year, also on the 10.30, and was not recorded at the time. However, Mr. M.S. King was a passenger on that train, and has kindly given an account of what occurred:

> 'The train divided behind the third coach near Weston Box (north of Winchester). I was standing in the corridor of the first vehicle at the time, and the sudden brake application - from 88 mph so I had estimated just previously - sent me into the front bulkhead of the coach with such force that my shoulder and right arm were jarred and I could hardly write for the next three days! After about 45 minutes' delay, we backed on to the remaining nine vehicles - which had stopped about 200 yards behind - coupled up (possibly using screw couplings) and proceeded slowly to Southampton Central where the front three coaches were removed. Unfortunately I was unable to find out the cause of this 'incident'; at the time I was only 14 years old and my enquiries were fobbed off with an answer to the order of "Get back to your seat!"'

It does seem that maintenance standards at this period were dropping off - along with everything else. One reason for the rapid run-down of Bulleid stock, and its quick withdrawal, was that the authorities feared that the timber-framed bodies would fare badly in an accident if BR all-steel stock was leading and trailing Bulleid carriages. They seem also to have been great rust-traps, as the later restorers have found; and probably this too speeded their demise.

At last on 10 July, 1967, the full electric service started, using mainly push-and-pull units without locomotives. However, there were still a few locomotive-hauled services, apart from the Waterloo-Exeter trains. There were the Southampton boat trains; the Channel Islands boat trains; the Weymouth Postal; and assorted newspaper and local trains that ran in the early hours. The boat trains were supposed to be composed of air-braked BR stock hauled by electro-diesel locomotives - but no locomotives were ready and few carriages had been converted to air-braking. So quite a few Bulleid coaches were kept on for several months for these duties, hauled by steam-heat-fitted Brush Type 4 diesel locomotives. The occasional SR coach could

Birmingham Railway Carriage & Wagon Co. built 3-coach Set S801; Third Brake S4222 is nearest. The small window next to the guard's door indicates a coupé compartment. Dated '6/48'.

*Eastleigh Carriage Works*

2-coach set for Waterloo-West of England services No. S 74, dated on solebar '5/48'. Corridor Third Brake S4382 and Corridor Brake Composite 6711.

*Eastleigh Carriage Works*

Corridor Brake Composite (loose stock) No. S6718, dated 6/48; the lavatory is in centre instead of the end.    *Eastleigh Carriage Works*

Painted in crimson lake and cream, the earliest BR standard coach livery; Corridor Composite No. S5857, for Set 839.

*Eastleigh Carriage Works*

'Loose' Corridor Third of 1950, probably No. S54, when new. In crimson and cream livery, the number is in the left-hand position, long water tank in roof.

*Eastleigh Carriage Works*

Two views of the remarkable plywood-bodied sleeping car, on 15th May 1949 .

*John L. Smith*

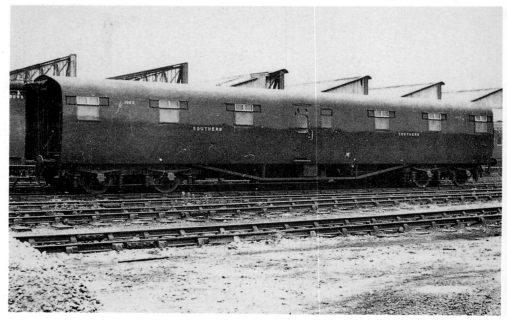

The Generator Van which was converted from ex-SECR luggage van (SR 1987) for use with the sleeping car; renumbered 97S and rebuilt with plywood body to the same profile.

*Lens of Sutton*

No. 7894 as rebuilt in 1959 as a kitchen/buffet car; here shown formed in the 'Surrey Downsman' special train at Oxted, 5th March, 1967                 *D. Gould*

The final duty for Dining First No. 7679 on a special run from Droxford to Knowle Junction on 13 May, 1966 headed by 'Terrier' No. 32646.  A stop was made at Wickham, as shown here                                 *R.W. Kidner*

also be seen in the Waterloo-Exeter sets, sometimes as extra stock, sometimes in place of the booked BR equivalent vehicle. One of the odder wanderings was that of Composite Brake 6727, which found itself in a temporary forma- tion on the Oxted line - which it had probably never before visited - between 21 July and 27 September, 1967. This 'scratch set' was a real oddity: it includ- ed five BR non-corridor coaches and a BR open first, and was standing in for set 701 (made up from former electric vehicles, but hauled just like an ordi- nary train), which was in shops being painted blue. Trains worked were the 17.20 London Bridge to Crowborough and the 7.57 Up service. Also note- worthy was the appearance of 2nd Bke 4353 and Compo 5722 as extra coach- es on the 10.12 Brighton to Exeter train on 22 July 1967, and of corridor 2nd 52 and open 2nd 1478 on the 12.15 Exeter to Brighton the same day.

Surviving Bulleid coaches after July 1967 included about 25 corridor 2nds, 21 open 2nds, 34 corridor brake 2nds, 22 corridor composites, 7 corr. bke. compos, 2 restaurant first saloons, two corridor firsts, 4 kitchen/buffet cars and 3 restaurant compo. saloons. More were condemned in October, when there was less need for extra coaches.

The various sidings were still being occupied by condemned stock, and in July and August 1967 the following were observed:-

At Oatlands - 35, 37/8, 66, 69, 91, 101, 121, 126, 1494, 1932, 4353, 4264, 3976, 3996/7, 2518, 5710, 5714, 5800. Corridor Second No. 66 was damaged in a shunting accident at Oatlands in August 1967 (after it had been with- drawn and sent there for disposal) and was cut up on site during September.

At Barnes - 47, 70, 83, 3995, 5802, 5872, 5922.

At Twickenham - 56, 92, 1506, 3960, 5773, 5888, 5892, 5895, 5910.

At Clapham Junction - 36, 50, 54, 61, 81, 99, 111, 1490, 1729/30, 2844, 4315, 4336, 4378, 3957, 2511, 5812, 5870, 5883, 5887, 7896.

Second Brakes Nos. 4365-7, withdrawn in 1966, were sent to Long Marston in November 1967 as RCT 1, 2 and 3 for the War Department depot there. Later they were renumbered W.D. 5200-2, and at least two were in continuous use there on 7 October 1972 when the Industrial Railway Society paid a visit. By then, the lower portion of the bodyside panels had been cut away. The subsequent history of 4366/7 is unknown, but it seems that No. 4365 must have been sent to the Army depot at Bicester, for it was from there that it was purchased by the Swanage Railway Society: it arrived at Swanage in March 1978 - oddly enough, still in BR green with the number 'S 4365 S' still painted on.

During 1968, it became much harder to observe Bulleid coaches in traffic on the Southern Region, and by the summer, almost the only type that was left was the open second - there were 13 of these in May 1968. The only other survivors after May were five Composites: 5740, 5761, 5768, 5857 and 5860. By now, the air-braked 8-sets for Ocean Liner trains (61 to 66) were ready,

and they also had locomotives to haul them; but the vacuum-braked sets were being worked so hard that failures were frequent and, there being virtually no spare sets, it was clearly found desirable to have a 'back-up' fleet of Bulleid stock to substitute for coaches withdrawn for maintenance. Things must have been bad on Saturday, 27th April, 1968, for, instead of the booked formation of ten blue-and-grey BR coaches on the 11.00 from Waterloo to Salisbury, it was a 10-coach train of all-green stock that turned up, a very rare sight at that late date. It included six Bulleid vehicles: open 2nds 1452, 1463, 1475, 1483 and 1453, and composite 5860; the other vehicles, B.R. second brakes S34233/4, open first S3514, and Gresley Buffet S9119 E, were also all due for quick withdrawal.

My own final ride in a Bulleid coach on British Rail was on 8th June, 1968, in No. 1504; this, with 1496, 1481, 1492, 1451 and 1464, was included in the formation of a special train named, appropriately enough, The Bulleid Commemorative Rail Tour. It was hauled from Waterloo to Seaford by one of his electric locomotives, 20002; and on via Brighton and Havant to Liss, where steam traction took over for a run to Longmoor and back over the Military Railway. The final section of the trip, from Guildford to Waterloo via Clandon, was with electric locomotive 20001.

And so the Bulleid saga on the Southern came to a close. The remaining vehicles were condemned between October and December 1968; those on the Eastern and Scottish Regions lasted a year or so longer. Comparatively few were converted to Departmental vehicles, and details of these are:-

| | |
|---|---|
| 1454: | To DS 70293 Test Coach c.1969. Wdn. 6.1972; to Morriston for scrap, 5/73. |
| 1456: | To DS 70285, c. 1967. To Bluebell Railway, 1980 |
| 1457: | To DS 70262, 3.1967 Tunnel Inspection Staff Coach. |
| | Still existing, 1985. |
| 4211: | To DS 70319, 1970. Carriage & Wagon Training Coach. Sold to Mid-Hants Railway, 3/76. |
| 4227: | To DW 150385, on Western Region, c.1966. To Bluebell Railway, 1987. |
| 4279: | To DS 70248, 4/66. Teleprinter Office, Eastleigh. Sold to Bluebell Railway, 7/70. |
| 4281: | Underframe to 080629, Lancing Works, c.1956. |
| 4008: | To DS 70251,1966 Inspection Coach. |
| | Still existing, 1985. |
| 2526: | To 082232 Internal user, date unknown. 'Newhaven'. Converted 4/74 at Stewarts Lane to ADB 975375 MEs RSE Section Instruction Car. |
| | Still existing, 1985. |
| 6702: | To 082233 Internal, 8/64. |

Vehicles purchased for preservation out of capital stock:

1464      To Merchant Navy Locomotive Preservation Society, first at Liss, 4/70, then to South Eastern Steam Centre, Ashford, 1971; finally to Bluebell Railway, 1978.

1481:     To Bluebell Railway, 7/70.

1482:     To Bluebell Railway, 3/73.

1469:     To Keighley & Worth Valley Rly., 1970.

2515:     To Bluebell Railway 3/73. (Orig. wdn. 9/66.)

5761:     To Mr. H. Frampton-Jones, first at Liss, 6/70; then Ashford, c. 10/71 to 5/78; finally to Mid-Hants Railway, 11/78.

5768:     To Bulleid Society, first at Liss, 1970; then on Bluebell Rly., 9/71.

## INSPECTION SALOON No. 100 S

This remarkable vehicle was Bulleid's least-known carriage; despite its official designation, it was actually a sleeping car, although not for use of the general public.

It is said that no authority was obtained from the SR Board or Committee to build 100 S; nevertheless, construction went ahead at Lancing, and it was completed in July 1946. Its intended purpose was to take directors of the Company and senior officials on tours of inspection round the system.

There were eleven bedrooms plus attendant's room, arranged longitudinally in groups of three, with a central corridor running the length of the car and a cross-vestibule with external doors in the middle. On one side, adjacent to the cross-vestibule, there was a lavatory; and on the other side, a shower, which was installed at Mr. Bulleid's behest. Each bedroom was equipped with a washbasin.

The body was made entirely of plywood, the exterior panels being resin-bonded to the plywood body framing. Apparently this was merely to demonstrate an alternative method to steel panelling; but it was unsuccessful. The plywood warped badly when the coach was stored under a glass roof in direct sunlight.

The bogies were different from the SR standard, although the wheelbase was the same - 8 ft. Each bogie had two radial bearing pads, one at the leading and one at the trailing end of the bogie, 14 ft 2 in. apart. These helped to cut down the fore-and-aft pitching of the bogies, thus making for excellent riding qualities.

To go with the sleeping car, several other vehicles were converted or modified. A generator van was made, former SE&CR Passenger Luggage Van No. 1987 (built by Bristol C.&W. Co. in 1921) forming the basis. The body of this was panelled over with plywood to give it a similar profile to

100 S, and a generator was installed. This would have been needed to sup-ply electricity for the saloon when in use and berthed in some siding during the night. The van was renumbered 97 S and was rebuilt in July 1946. Two Maunsell dining cars were appropriated in July 1948 to make up the mobile 'hotel': these were 7940 (renumbered 98 S) and 7943 (99 S), both of which had been improved internally in 1938 for the 'Bournemouth Limited' service and were thus up to the standard required for use by 'top brass'. Finally, one of the luxurious Maunsell Nondescript Brake coaches, No. 4444 of 1933, was used in the train, presumably as a drawing room, and renumbered 444 S.

How many outings the saloon made is not known, although Lord Hurcomb, the first Chairman of BR, once travelled in it and was most impressed with the riding qualities. *The Railway Magazine* (Vol. 95 p. 416) noted that No. 100 S was worked to Salisbury on the 2.50 pm passenger train from Waterloo on 23rd August, 1949, on a running test after renewal of its springs, and was returned to Waterloo on the 4.50 pm. It was stated that the vehicle by 1949 was used on inspection trips by principal officers. It was usu-ally stabled at Stewarts Lane depot.

It seems that there was a prohibition on the taking of photographs: one person doing this on one occasion was asked officially to destroy his nega-tive. Presumably the saloon gradually fell into disuse, and later was hidden away in sidings at Lancing; it was stripped in 1955 and set on fire in 1956; the underframe also was destroyed, and Southern Carriage & Wagon Society members found no trace of it. The generator van was withdrawn in December 1957, but lingered on at Eastleigh as 081033, usually standing next to the 'aeroplane shed' until about 1960. The other three carriages were returned to capital stock with their original numbers, 7940 in 1951, and 4444 and 7943 in about 1956.

Official withdrawal date for 100 S was December 1953.

## NON-PASSENGER CARRYING VEHICLES*

### 4- WHEELED LUGGAGE VANS

Construction of the standard Maunsell-design luggage vans continued without interruption until 1947, and a final batch came out in 1951. The only variations were ten plastic-bodied vans - in which Bulleid certainly had a hand - and a large number of plywood-sheeted vehicles built in 1950. All luggage vans, except the plastic-bodied series, had the same general dimen-sions: 21 ft wheelbase, 35 ft 8 in. overall length, 32 ft body length, 7 ft 10 1/4 in. body width, and were 12 ft high. Under BR, they were re-classed as 'Parcels & Miscellaneous Vans'.

---

* A more detailed account of the vehicles covered in this section can be found in *Southern Railway Passenger Vans*, by David Gould, Oakwood Press, 1993.

ORDER No. 1092. Underframes built at Lancing, bodies at Eastleigh. 1940; vehicle Nos. 1821 to 1920. Planking (or sheeting) arranged horizontally in alternate pairs 3 1/2 in. and 6 1/2 in. wide. In the 1950s No. 1882 was fitted as a cycle van, distinguished by a stencilled bicycle in the top righthand corner of the body and equipped with 24 hooks; along with nine other cycle vans of pre-War construction, it worked in various Continental boat trains. Cycle vans were abolished after 1969.

Only eight of this batch had been withdrawn by 1978, two as the result of accident damage: No. 1919 in 1961, and 1889 which was damaged at Glasgow Queen Street on 2 Aug. 1975 and broken up on the spot. No. 1851 was sold to the Mid-Hants Railway in 1976. The rest were withdrawn by 1982.

ORDER No. 1191. Built at Lancing 1942; Nos. 1781 to 1820 and 2091 to 2170. The sheeting arrangement was peculiar to this batch, and comprised 6 1/2 in. wide planks, plus a narrow plank along the centre-line of the body. They also had 'U'-section steel strapping, with the timber bolted to one angle of the 'U'.

Rather oddly, some of these were converted to service vehicles after only five or six years in traffic; the normal choice for departmental stock were the earliest SR vans or the ex-SE&CR type. The following vans were converted:-

1787 to 466 S, c. 1948; 1791 to 469 S; 2127 to 470 S; 2164 to 471 S; all in 1947 for use in a weedkilling train, which included several tanks altered from locomotive tenders, and a couple of standard SR goods brake vans. DS 470 (as it became) withdrawn 1977. 2138 to DS 147 Staff & Tool Van in 1954.

Vans withdrawn after accidents: 2094 at Oxheys 20 Jan. 1970; 2098 at Bounds Green June 1960; and 2128 at West Ealing 26 Aug. 1972. Ten others had been condemned by 1979.

ORDER No. 1659. Built at Lancing in 1943; Nos. 1053, 1692 to 1730, and 2083 to 2090. Body sheeting, alternate pairs of 3 1/2 in. and 6 1/2 in. planks Nos. 1692 and 1720 transferred to the Isle of Wight in October 1950 and renumbered 1052 and 1048. On withdrawal in December 1966, both became 'Internal User' vans at Ryde, renumbered 082056 (ex 1720) and 082975 (ex 1692). When 082975 was finally condemned in March 1976, it was purchased by the Wight Locomotive Society and moved to the Isle of Wight Steam Railway at Haven Street on 27 May 1976.

No. 1728 became a cycle van, fitted with 60 hooks, for use in Continental boat trains in the 1950s; still so-equipped in 1966. Three of the pre-War luggage vans were aiso similarly-altered. No. 1709 was fitted with chains for BR Universal Trolleys some time before 1973 and allocated to specific services on the South Eastern Division.

ORDER No. 1659A Nos. 1401 to 1410; built 1943/4. These were the experimental luggage vans with plastic bodies, designed to reduce weight while still having the same carrying capacity as the conventional vans. Tare weight

was 10 tons 4 cwt compared with 13 tons of the standard vans; length over headstocks 33 ft; length over body 32 ft 2 5/8 in.; width over lock handles 8 ft 8 7/8 in.; rail to roof 12 ft 5 in.; and wheelbase was 22 ft.

The body on each of these vans was able to slide several inches longitudinally over the underframe against the resistance of a spring-cushioning device whenever braking or buffing effects might have otherwise caused a severe shock. Because of the spring-cushioning, it was possible to build both frame and body of lighter materials than normal; the need for heavy materials, necessary on conventional vehicles to withstand the compressive buffing forces, was obviated. The body was prevented from becoming detached from the frame by inwardly facing clips attached, two a side, to the main longitudinals of the underframe; the upper ends of these clips held the lower flanges of the outwardly-facing channel members forming part of the body floor. In addition to a 'Prestall' vacuum-brake cylinder, a handbrake was fitted. The body frame was made of light 12-gauge steel sections, 2 1/2 in. by 11 1/4 in. channel, electric-welded in a jig. The plastic panels, weighing 11 1/2 ounces per square foot, were reinforced by steel wire and cotton; these were used for sides, ends and roof; doors, however, were of light sheet steel less than 1 in. thick.

The design was not repeated; these ten vans were all that were built. Nos. 1401/10 were withdrawn by June 1963; 1405/6/8 by December 1963; and 1404/9 by June 1966. 1403 went in 1967, 1402 in 1972, and 1407 in 1966.

ORDER No. 3229. Built at Ashford, 1947; Nos. 1501 to 1560. These vans reverted to the standard 3 1/2 in./6 1/2 in. planked body and were to the same dimensions. In 1964, Nos. 1537 and 1558 were equipped with through wiring connections to permit working with electrically-heated carriages. From 6th June, 1966, they were booked to work in the 'Golden Arrow' service, one van at each end of the train; on the Down service, 10.30 from Victoria, the front van was for accompanied luggage and the rear van for registered luggage. When not in use the two vans were berthed at Stewarts Lane. In 1967 the vacuum brakes were replaced by air brakes, and the vans appeared on Oxted Line and Reading-Tonbridge passenger trains, these having become air-braked in that year. Unfortunately there was no further use for air-braked parcels vans after May 1973, and so they were packed off to Bristol (Western Region again!). But the WR couldn't make anything of them and both were condemned in 1976 - No. 1558 having been renumbered DB 975567 shortly before withdrawal. Nos. 1502 and 1516 were fitted with chains for BRUTE traffic on rostered services. By 1978 none of this batch had been withdrawn except Nos. 1537/58. The last were withdrawn in 1982.

ORDER No. 3590. Built by BR in 1950; Nos. 1561 to 1671. At Ashford: 1561-9/72/4-80/4-7/9/91/2/4-1608/12-9/23/9-32/46/7/59. Underframes at Ashford, bodies at Eastleigh: 1570/1/3/81-3/1609-11/20-2/24/5/53.

Underframes at Ashford, bodies at Lancing: 1588/90/3/1626-8/33-45/8-52, 1654-8/60-71. All this batch were fitted with plywood bodies, which gave them a 'cheap-and-nasty' appearance; however the doors were planked as on earlier vans. In about 1963, Nos. 1621 to 1625 were fitted to work with push and pull trains, replacing five similar vans (ex-SEC) which had been fitted since 1941. Nos. 1621-5 were all allocated to the South Western Division: push-and-pull worked branch lines included those to Swanage, Lymington, and Yeovil Town. With the cessation of steam-worked pull-and-push services, these vans reverted to the general pool.

Nos. 1562/76, 1613/8/28 were converted to security vans in November 1963 with steel sheet behind the windows; one set of doors each side was sealed. The vans appear to have reverted to standard by 1964. Nos. 1626 and 1647 were fitted with through connections for electric heating by June 1965, and air-braked in 1967; they worked on the Oxted and Reading-Tonbridge services until 1973, when they were sent to Bristol. No. 1626 became DB 975568 in 1976, and both were condemned that same year.

Vans withdrawn after accident damage: 1627, at Camden, Oct. 1974; 1657, at Norwood Yard - broken up there March 1977. Eight others had been condemned by 1979. Those remaining were withdrawn 1981-84.

The final series of SR-style luggage vans was built at BR Wolverton Works in 1951. Bodies reverted to the planked style with alternate pairs of 3 1/2 in. and 6 1/2 in.-wide planks. Numbers were 1451 to 1500.

No. 1454 became a cycle van, with 24 hooks, for Continental boat trains, until some time after 1969. Several of this batch were given through connections for electric heating: No. 1499 in 1965, and 1455, 1476, 1482, 1495 and 1496 a year later. All six had vacuum brakes removed and air brakes substituted in 1967.

From 10th July, 1967, the Monday to Friday workings of these, and the earlier vans fitted with electric wiring and air brakes, were as follows:-

| Working 484: | 6.25 | Victoria to Brighton via Ashurst and 18.53 return. Next day: No. 485. |
|---|---|---|
| Working 485: | 5.20 | Victoria to East Croydon; 15.55 to East Grinstead and to Yard; 20.31 E. Grinstead to Victoria. Next day: No. 484. |
| Working 487 and 488 (2 vans): | 6.49 | Reading to Redhill (not Mons.); 18.41 to Tonbridge (not Mons.); 19.46 Tonbridge to Reading. |
| Working 489: | 16.40 | Redhill to Reading, 23.24 Reading to Guildford; 0.21 Vans and empty stock to Redhill. |

They were used primarily for conveying mails.

After closure of the Uckfield-Lewes section of line, air-braked parcels vans no longer appeared on Oxted Line passenger trains, but there were still

three regular workings on Reading-Tonbridge locomotive-hauled trains until May 1973; the vans were then replaced by BR standard bogie General Utility Vans, which were more capacious. The SR vans, 1455/76/82/95/6/9, were transferred to the Western Region in June 1973, like the others official-ly 'on loan' - but they never returned. All but two were condemned in 1976 (No. 1496 having been renumbered DB 975566 in the B.R. series of depart-mental vehicles); the final two - 1455 and 1495 - were withdrawn in about September 1977. Only five other vans in this series had gone by 1979 - Nos. 1460,1463,1471 (which was damaged at Camden in August 1974), 1475 and 1498. All the rest went in 1981-84.

## COVERED CARRIAGE TRUCKS (4-WHEELED)

The last vans of this type built by the Southern Railway came out in 1938; but the design was revived as late as 1951 and several more were built. Dimensions were the same as the pre-War version: 35 ft 10 in. overall length, 32 ft. 4 1/4 in. body length, 8 ft 10 7/8 in. maximum width, and 12 ft from rail to roof. Wheelbase was 21 ft. The main difference between the B R-built vehicles and the SR type was that the newer vans had plywood bodysides; the doors, however, had alternate pairs of 3 1/2 in. and 6 1/2 in.-wide planks.

ORDER No. 3702. Built at Ashford, 1951; Nos. 1411 to 1450, 1977 to 1991, 2006 to 2020, 2073 to 2082, 2171 to 2180, and 2231 to 2240. The reason for the short runs of consecutive numbers was clearly that gaps left by earlier vehi-cles were now being filled. Most of this batch were still in existence in 1979; 1412 was withdrawn after fire damage in November 1973, 2020 was burnt out at Roade on 3rd October, 1972, and 2018 was sold in 1978 to the Central Wagon Co., Ince. Nos. 1979 and 2234 had also been withdrawn. The remain-der went in 1981-86.

ORDER No. 3764. Built at Lancing, 1955; Nos. 2501 to 2550. These were the last 4-wheeled covered carriage trucks to the SR design to be built; the design must have been very highly thought of at this late date, for the first vehicles had appeared in 1928, and the 1955 batch differed only in having plywood bodysides. No. 2523 was damaged at Horsham in May 1958; 2541 at Desborough on 3 July 1963; otherwise, only 2538 had gone by 1978. However all the rest were withdrawn between 1981 and 1986.

## 4-WHEELED GUARD'S VANS

Once again, the pre-War design of these vans was continued without a break during Bulleid's regime, although no more were built after 1941. Overall length of each vehicle was 39 ft 8 in. and body length 36 ft; maximum width 8 ft. 10 7/8 in. and height to roof centre 12 ft. There was a central

guard's compartment flanked by two luggage compartments each 15 ft 5 1/2 in. long. Wheelbase 23 ft and weight 16 tons.

ORDER No. 1090. Underframes built at Lancing, bodies at Eastleigh, 1940/1; Nos. 931 to 980. In the 1950s, Nos. 937, 943, 952, 956, 961, 966, 972 and 979 were fitted with roof boards lettered 'Newspaper Traffic'; by September 1960 Nos. 961 and 972 were no longer so distinguished, and two of the vehicles were in traffic with four spare. One of the 4-wheeled vans - coded 'News BY' by BR - was booked to be included in the 3.17 am Salisbury to Weymouth and 11.30 Weymouth to Waterloo, both workings being Tuesdays to Saturdays and each van running on alternate days. By 1964, 4-wheeled vans were no longer in use for newspaper traffic.

Several vans were withdrawn in late 1968 and 1969, and by 1973 the guard's compartments were out of use, the vans being gloomily labelled 'No Lighting'; they were now regarded as merely parcel vans. Withdrawal continued steadily, and the last (933, 947, 950, 957, 959, 966, 968, 972 and 975) were condemned in July 1978. Many were sold to scrap merchants, but No. 931, withdrawn early in 1978, was acquired by the Llangollen Railway Society for preservation.

ORDER No. 1091 Underframes built at Lancing, bodies at Eastleigh, 1941. Each of these vans was fitted with a safe, which extended the width of the vehicle, with a small external door on each bodyside. On these vans, the guard's compartment was 7ft 3 in. long instead of only 4 ft 6 in. , resulting in a smaller luggage compartment at one end of the van, 12 ft 8 1/2in. long. The other luggage compartment, which included the safe, was 15 ft 5 1/2 in. long as usual. The vans weighed 15 tons each, and were distinguished by the vehicle number being painted in large white figures on a red panel.

Withdrawals: 10, 11/76; 11, 12/77; 12, 7/78; 13, 4/78; 14, 9/69.

## BOGIE GUARD'S VANS

The last of this type built by the Southern Railway were in 1939; but the design was revived as late as 1952, and 30 more were constructed. They measured 50 ft over headstocks and 53 ft 8 in. overall; periscope 12 ft 8 in. The central guard's compartment was 4 ft 6 in.

ORDER No. 3227. Built at Lancing, 1952/3; Nos. 251 to 280. In the 1950s, Nos. 265 to 280 were roofboarded 'Newspaper Traffic' for use on the Western Section. Workings for the 'News Vans B', from 12 September, 1960, were:

| | |
|---|---|
| 1.15 am | W'loo to Padstow; 3.13 pm Padstow to Exeter Ctl.; 6.48 pm. Perishables Exeter to Clapham Jn. |
| 1.15 am | W'loo to Torrington; 8.53 am (until 29.10.60) or 10.30 am (31.10.60 until 29.4.61) Torrington to Exeter; 11.45 am or 1.45 pm Exeter to Exmouth; 4.0 pm Exmouth to Waterloo (freight from Sidmouth Jn.). |

| | |
|---|---|
| 1.15 am | W'loo to Exeter Ctl.; 5.21 am Exeter to Torrington; 8.53 am (until 29.10.60) or 10.30 am (31.10.60 to 29.4.61) Torrington to Exeter Ctl.; 11.47 am Exeter to Bude and 3.17 pm to W'loo (until 29.10.60) or 4.30 pm Exeter to W'loo (31.10.60 to 29.4.61). |
| 3.20 am | Salisbury to Yeovil Town and 4.6 pm to Waterloo. |
| 1.15 am | W'loo to Exeter; 5.21 am to Ilfracombe; 3.0 pm Ilf. to W'loo. |
| 3.17 am | Salisbury to Weymouth; 8.25 am to Bournemouth; 4.55 pm to W'loo. |
| 1.15 am | W'loo to Yeovil Town and 8.10 pm return. |

To work these seven diagrams were needed 14 vans, as each vehicle worked on alternate days, and there were also two vans standing spare.

By 1964, vans were no longer roof boarded, merely stencilled 'Newspaper Traffic', and only Nos. 272 to 280 were so marked. By 1973, like the 4-wheeled vans, they no longer had accommodation for guard, being re-classed Parcels and Miscellaneous Vans. By May 1975, Nos. 278 to 280 were taken off newspaper traffic duties; and by May 1977 only Nos. 276 and 277 were still stencilled 'Newspaper Traffic' and were now booked to work between Victoria and Hastings/Bexhill. Rather remarkably, not a single example of this 251-280 series had been withdrawn at the end of 1978, but all were gone by 1986.

## 'PRESERVED' BULLEID COACHES

Of the thirteen post-war Southern steam-hauled carriages now in private ownership, no fewer than eight are to be found on the Bluebell Railway. An enormous amount of time has been spent on their renovation; all had arrived on the line in more-or-less poor condition, but by April 1979 four had been restored, externally and internally, to gleaming condition.

The first two vehicles to be acquired were Open Third 1481 of 1950 and BRC&W-built Third Brake 4279 of 1949. No. 1481 had stood at Coulsdon North for over a year since its withdrawal from BR service in August 1968 and was moved to Micheldever in November 1969. No. 4279 had been con-verted to DS 70248 Teleprinter Office and both the seating and the partition between the two end compartments had been removed. This coach had been in use at Rotherhithe Road (the carriage shed was still in existence at that time). Both coaches were sent to Stewarts Lane for partial overhaul and repainting in Southern Railway livery. They were then worked from Norwood Yard to Haywards Heath on 20th June, 1970, and taken by road thence to Sheffield Park during July. Replacement seating for 4279 was obtained from a '6-COR' Motor Saloon Brake car. For the first time in the Bluebell's history, a train set was formed using all buckeye-coupled stock: it was numbered 23, and comprised these two vehicles in malachite green, plus Maunsell Open Third 1365 and Corridor Brake Composite 6575; this set was

first used on 'The Decadian', 10th Anniversary Day, 2nd August, 1970.

The initial 'restoration' of No. 4279 was not entirely satisfactory. Although seating for the two end compartments had been found (taken from 2-HAL electric stock at Selhurst), the partition was still missing, so that riding in one of these 'compartments' reminded one of Victorian carriages with their half-height partitions. A handbrake was missing from the guard's compartment, and the bogies were transposed; an unwary guard climbing down and expecting to find a footboard on the bogie at the brake-end would step into empty air. This serious defect was remedied in April 1973, and the bogies were swapped to their correct ends. 4279 was also fitted with a handbrake in 1973, and the following year equipped with electric lighting. However, it was clear that the coach needed serious attention, and so was withdrawn on 12th September, 1976. Many of the main body timbers were found to be rotten when the coach was stripped down to its framework, part of which was replaced using sections specially made at Sheffield Park sawmill. All the temporary fittings were replaced, including the handbrake column, seating, and lighting. The compartment partition was reinstated at last. On 14th April, 1979, No. 4279 emerged from Horsted Keynes carriage shed in superb condition, painted in SR livery and with the set number '820' on the end.

No. 1481 has had plenty of use since 1970. The brake gear was overhauled in 1975, and the coach received reconditioned bogies from a withdrawn Bulleid restaurant car in 1976.

The third coach to arrive on the line, Composite 5768, is not owned by the Bluebell Railway but by the Bulleid Society. It was purchased in 1968 and went to Liss in about 1970; but as part of a large transfer of stock it was moved by rail from Liss to Haywards Heath on 27th September, 1971, the final part of the journey being by road three days later. After some years of standing in the open, No. 5768 was in poor condition and soon sought the shelter of Horsted Keynes carriage shed where work on it started. It made its first passenger trip on the line on 26th May, 1974, although not completed; most of the interior had been renovated, and the roof given a new canvas covering. The coach was thoroughly restored and sent into traffic on 15th May, 1976; but unfortunately it had to be hastily withdrawn again as three of the large windows had cracked, owing to a build-up of rust in their frames which distorted them, resulting in uneven pressure on the glass. It was found that some parts of the window frames had corroded right away. Further repairs to the Composite took a year; it was stated that the damage had been caused by water leaking through the cantrail during the time the coach was stored in the open and penetrating behind the body panels of which large sections were rusted through. These had to be cut out and new sections welded in. No. 5768 was finally outshopped on 8th May, 1977.

Third Brake No. 2515 had spent a great deal of time at Micheldever Sidings following its withdrawal in 1966. It had been retained for conversion to a Gauging Van, but this was not done, and the intact coach was offered for sale in 1970. It was not possible to purchase it immediately, but eventually this was done and the coach was moved to Haywards Heath late in 1972 and transferred to Sheffield Park on 2nd March, 1973. This coach needed very heavy repairs. Much of the body timber was rotten and had to be replaced; the new main-frame timbering, 9 in. by 4 in. on a 12 ft 9 in. radius curve, had to be specially ordered. The pressed-steel doors had accumulated so much rust that they were rejected in favour of doors off scrapped 4-SUB electric units, some being made of fibreglass. Seating was reupholstered in a type of red-and-black striped moquette that was in vogue on BR during the late 1960s. The steam heating was restored. A great amount of work was done in the area round the lavatory, where the roof covering was in the worst condition. The coach entered revenue service on 6th February, 1977; in particular, the finish of the interior was magnificent, and it was noticed that, in true Lancing Works style, all the screw-heads were in line with the grain of the woodwork! By 1979, the set number '820' had appeared on the brake-end, and this coach, with 4279 and 5768, was scheduled to operate in a 3-set as in Southern practice.

The fifth coach to arrive on the Bluebell was Open Third No. 1482. This vehicle had been sent to Scotland, painted in BR lined maroon livery, and after withdrawal became a mess room at Bellahouston carriage sheds, Glasgow, where it was 'discovered' by the Scottish Railway Preservation Society, who, hoping to get the Bluebell's Caledonian Railway corridor coach in return, offered it to the Sussex concern. It was accepted, and made the journey south, eventually arriving at Haywards Heath on 24th February, 1973, and on by road on 3rd March, 1973, only one day after No. 2515. No. 1482 went straight into service, running in its maroon livery until after Easter that year; then it went in for heavy overhaul. It was given a completely new floor, and the underframe and bogies were scraped clean to the bare metal before being painted. Like all other Bulleid coaches on this line, regardless of origin, it was painted in Southern Railway malachite green livery, lettered 'Southern'. Restoration complete, the coach entered traffic on 15th May, 1976.

A further Bulleid Third Brake was acquired in 1977, not for preservation but as a source of spares. It was No. 4036, ex Chipman Chemical Company CWT 12, and it was transported by road from Horsham to the railway on 16th and 17th June, 1977. It presented a curious appearance in its Chipman red and white livery, standing off rails at the back of Horsted Keynes carriage shed; after a few years the body was scrapped.

Yet another Open Third arrived on the line: No. 1464, in 1978. This was originally acquired by the Merchant Navy Locomotive Preservation Society,

and travelled from Micheldever to Liss in April 1970. When the various societies gathered there were told to leave, the MNLPS transferred its stock to the South Eastern Steam Centre at the former Ashford locomotive shed in about August or September 1971. Unfortunately this jolly little gathering was equally-abruptly broken up as British Rail claimed non-payment of rent by the man running the Centre; the MNLPS hurried its locomotive off to Hereford, but left the rolling stock to its fate. The Bluebell-based Southern Coaching Stock Group managed to acquire No. 1464, and it came to the line in 1978. It was still in BR green livery, and was unusual in still having four rainstrips on the roof. Restoration was completed in April 1986.

A fourth Open Third, No. 1456, was delivered to the Bluebell on 11th August, 1980, on loan from the National Railway Museum of York, which had claimed it on its withdrawal as DS 70285. This was one of the vehicles with 'skirted' bodyside panels and, although badly rusted when it arrived at Horsted Keynes, it was descibed by the carriage and wagon foreman as 'remarkably complete. . . it looks far worse than it really is.' It had not been restored by 1994, when it still wore the green applied by Lancing in May 1963!

From Bristol in April 1987 came Third Brake No. 4227, which had been a departmental vehicle on the Western Region since about 1966 as DW 150385. This is one of two surviving Birmingham-built Bulleid coaches that incorporated a coupé compartment next to the guard's compartment. Although No. 4227 had been gutted, the Bluebell stated that it had sufficient seating in stock to enable future restoration, which had not occurred by 1994.

By 1979, the Mid-Hants Railway, which had the disadvantage of a late start, had gathered together three Bulleid carriages. The first to arrive at Alresford was Third Brake No. 4211, one of the BRC&W-built series with coupé compartments. This was worked in a special train from Alton on 6th March, 1976, the only train to run over the Alton-Ropley section since closure on 5th February, 1973; track was lifted soon afterwards. The track was relaid during 1982-84 and through services between Alton and Ropley began in 1985. No. 4211, which had been gutted, was converted into a static refreshment car; the place where the two compartments once were became a service area and staff room, and the saloon, which was fitted with seats and tables taken from a BR open second as the original seating had been stripped when the coach was a service vehicle (DS 70319), was ideally suited as a refreshment room. The former lavatory compartment was used as a store. The coach was painted in a pleasant light green, but without number or identity of owner. It was gas-fitted for boiling water, and was stationed at Alresford. A refrigerator was installed in the former luggage compartment. No. 4211 was in traffic, painted in BR green, by 1989.

1947-built corridor composite No. 5761 was the next to arrive, on 23rd

November, 1978. This coach was 'rescued' in May 1978 from Ashford loco-motive shed, where it had stood since 1971, and uncared-for since the South Eastern Steam Centre (as the shed was known) was forced to close. The owner is Mr. H. Frampton-Jones. By October 1979 new canvas had been applied to the roof and some painting had been carried out.

The only survivor of the Bulleid 59 ft stock is Corridor Third Brake No. 2850; this was acquired from the Chipman Chemical Company of Horsham. Certainly it is an interesting vehicle, although even in November 1976 it seemed in very poor condition externally, and had probably been out of use for some time. With the Bluebell's experience in mind of how rapidly Bulleid coaches deteriorate, and the fact that up to 1979 there was no cover of any kind for carriages on the Mid-Hants Railway, one fears that many disagree-able surprises await the carriage restorers.

Southerners have a long way to go to see Open Third No. 1469, for this example is to be found on the Keighley & Worth Valley Railway in West Yorkshire. Curiously enough, this was about the first Bulleid coach to be preserved. The Vintage Carriage Trust obtained it at Bishops Stortford in 1969, and it made the journey north during the following year. Subsequently, it appears from published photographs to have seen plenty of use.

The Swanage Railway Society purchased Third Brake No. 4365 from the Army depot near Bicester and it arrived at Swanage Station site in March 1978. The Society had very little track, but it did have the use of a large goods shed, and happily this is where the coach was stored. About 1/4 mile of track had been laid out of Swanage by August 1979, and passenger carrying was begun, using the Bulleid coach. By October, it was once again safely in the goods shed, and repainting in malachite green was well advanced. Fortunately, No. 4365 was in very good condition, and all the seating was intact; even the steam-heating controls were still there. One of the window frames, that in the compartment nearest the guard's compartment, was severely corroded at the base; but that is a failing common to most other Bulleid carriages. No. 4365 has seen use on passenger train services.

Strictly speaking, Dining First No. 7679 was not 'preserved', but nor was it sold for scrap, so it is difficult to decide under which heading to place it. The vehicle was in fact sold in about 1965 to a rather secret concern with a base at Droxford Station, on the closed Meon Valley line. The portion of line from Knowle Junction to Droxford was leased from British Rail (including Wickham Station), in connection with the development of the Sadler Rail Coach - a luxuriously-appointed vehicle which could have had a great future on branchlines - and stationed at Droxford. The first attempt to fetch No. 7679 from Knowle Junction was not successful. Mr. May, who was the man-ager at Droxford, raised steam on 0-6-0T No. 32646 (which had been pur-

chased in June 1964) specially to pick up the dining car at Knowle Junction one day; but BR had failed to deliver it. Meanwhile, evil hands had jammed a piece of wood in facing points, and, on the way back to Droxford, the engine derailed at the obstruction. The manager's annoyance at a futile journey culminating in a derailment may be imagined, and it was some weeks before he could go down again to pick up the coach.

Mr. May used No. 7679 as a lounge, and it stood alongside the station building at Droxford.

On Friday, 13th May, 1966, a non-stop champagne party took place in the dining car, which was propelled from Droxford to Knowle and hauled back by No. 32646. The party was presided over by Sir Rupert Brickwood and celebrated the locomotive's last run in steam before becoming an outsize inn-sign at South Hayling; Sadler no longer required the engine and had sold it to Brickwood's. The party was held in the saloon part of No. 7679; it is likely that a few of the chairs were removed to make room for the large supplies of champagne. The gangway door at the locomotive end was left open and, by clambering round the coal bunker, participants were able to alternate between tippling and footplate riding.

After this excitement, nothing more was reported, and visitors were not encouraged. The whole scheme seems to have faded away, and the dining car was burnt in about 1968, the remains having been discovered at about that time. What a tragedy that this most interesting vehicle was not re-sold to one of the preservation societies!

## Disposition and Withdrawal Dates of Bulleid Corridor Coaches

The following lists shows coach numbers and the sets in which each vehicle was placed until the abolition of sets in March 1966: all surviving coaches from that date were 'loose'. The date following each set number is that of the vehicle's first appearance in the set concerned, according to the Appendices to Carriage Working Notices. 'L' indicates a loose coach, shown only up to 1965.

### Corridor Thirds

| | | | | | | Wdn. |
|---|---|---|---|---|---|---|
| 26 | 80 | 5/49 | | | | 8.67 |
| 27 | 81 | 5/49; L 6/63; | 63 | 6/65 | | 1.68 |
| 28 | 82 | 5/49; L 6/63; | 768 | 6/64 | | 7.67 |
| 29 | 83 | 5/49; L 6/63; | 803 | 6/64 | | 10.67 |
| 30 | 84 | 5/49; L 6/63; | 803 | 6/64 | | 9.67 |
| 31 | 85 | 5/49; L 6/63; | 964 | 6/65 | | 6.67 |
| 32 | 86 | 5/49; L 6/63 | | | | 2.65 |
| 33 | 87 | 5/49; L 6/63; | 803 | 6/64 | | 8.67 |
| 34 | 88 | 5/49; L 6/63; | 981 | 6/65 | | 7.67 |
| 35 | 89 | 5/49; L 6/63; | 981 | 6/65 | | 7.67 |
| 36 | 90 | 5/49; L 6/63; | 981 | 6/65 | | 8.67 |
| 37 | 91 | 5/49; L 6/63; | 803 | 6/64 | | 7.67 |
| 38 | 92 | 5/49; L 6/63; | 984 | 6/65 | | 8.67 |
| 39 | 93 | 5/49; L 6/63; | 976 | 6/64 | | 12.67 |
| 40 | 94 | 5/49; L 6/63; | 984 | 6/65 | | 7.66 |
| 41 | 265 | 6/50; L 6/59; | 897 | 11/59; | | |
| | | L 6/64; | 984 | 6/65 | | 7.67 |
| 42 | 265 | 6/50; L 6/59; | 897 | 11/59; | | |
| | | L 6/64 | | | | 7.67 |
| 43 | 267 | 6/50; L 6/59; | 897 | 11/59; | | |
| | | L 6/64; | 69 | 6/65 | | 12.65 |
| 44 | 267 | 6/50; L 6/59; | 823 | 6/63; | | |
| | | L 6/64 | | | | 7.67 |
| 45 | 267 | 6/50; L 6/59; | 80 | 6/61; | | |
| | | | 804 | 6/62 | | 7.67 |
| 46 | 266 | 6/50; L 6/63; | 976 | 6/64 | | 7.67 |
| 47 | 266 | 6/50; L 6/63; | 967 | 6/64 | | 8.67 |
| 48 | 266 | 6/50; L 6/63; | 976 | 6/64 | | 8.67 |
| 49 | 266 | 6/50; L 6/63; | 976 | 6/64 | | 7.67 |
| 50 | 266 | 6/50; L 6/61; | 824 | 6/63; | | |
| | | | 807 | 6/64; | | |
| | | | 804 | 6/65 | | 7.67 |
| 51 | | L 6/50; | 874 | 6/53; | | |
| | | L 6/63; | 968 | 6/64 | | 6.67 |
| 52 | | L 6/50; | 874 | 6/53; | | |
| | | L 6/63; | 968 | 6/64 | | 11.67 |
| 53 | | L 6/50; | 874 | 6/53; | | |
| | | L 6/63; | 968 | 6/64 | | 7.67 |
| 54 | | L 6/50; | 876 | 6/53; | | |
| | | | 804 | 6/62 | | 8.67 |
| 55 | 264 | 6/50; L 6/63; | 968 | 6/64 | | 7.67 |
| 56 | 264 | 6/50; L 6/63; | | | | 8.67 |
| 57 | 838 | 6/50; | | | | 10.67 |
| 58 | 838 | 6/50; | | | | 7.67 |
| 59 | 839 | 6/50; | | | | 10.67 |

| | | | Wdn. |
|---|---|---|---|
| 60 | 839 | 6/50; | 11.67 |
| 61 | 840 | 6/50; | 8.67 |
| 62 | 840 | 6/50; | 5.67 |
| 63 | 841 | 6/50; | 7.67 |
| 64 | 841 | 6/50; | 3.67 |
| 65 | 842 | 6/50; | 9.66 |
| 66 | 842 | 6/50; | 7.67 |
| 67 | 843 | 6/50; | 7.67 |
| 68 | 843 | 6/50; | 10.66 |
| 69 | 844 | 6/50; | 7.67 |
| 70 | 844 | 6/50; | 9.67 |
| 71 | 845 | 6/50; | 5.67 |
| 72 | 845 | 6/50; | 7.67 |
| 73 | 846 | 6/50; | 8.67 |
| 74 | 846 | 6/50; | 7.66 |
| 75 | 847 | 6/50; | 12.65 |
| 76 | 847 | 6/50; | 7.67 |
| 77 | 848 | 6/50; | 8.67 |
| 78 | 848 | 6/50; | 5.67 |
| 79 | 849 | 6/50; | 7.67 |
| 80 | 849 | 6/50, | 5.66 |
| 81 | L; 473 6/54; L 6/59; 264 2/61; | | |
| | L 6/63; 836 6/64 | | 7.67 |
| 82 | L; 473 6/54; L 6/59; 264 2/61; | | |
| | L 6/63, 832 6/65 | | 12.67 |
| 83 | L; 473 6/54; L 6/59; 824 6/63; | | |
| | 807 6/64; L 6/65 | | 7.67 |
| 84 | L; 875 6/53; 825 6/63; 808 6/64 | | 1.68 |
| 85 | L; 474 6/54; 980 6/65 | | 10.67 |
| 86 | L; 474 6/54; 980 6/65 | | 8.67 |
| 87 | L; 474 6/54; 980 6/65 | | 7.67 |
| 88 | L; 875 6/53; 803 11/61; 804 6/64 | | 1.68 |
| 89 | L; 875 6/53; 803 11/61; 804 6/64 | | 1.68 |
| 90 | L; 474 6/54; 964 6/65 | | 8.67 |
| 91 | L; 873 6/55; L 6/63; 70 6/65 | | 7.67 |
| 92 | L; 802 6/55; 474 6/64; 964 6/65 | | 8.67 |
| 93 | L; 767 6/55; L 6/64; 769 6/65 | | 7.67 |
| 94 | L; 767 6/55; L 6/64; 769 6/65 | | 1.67 |
| 95 | L; 767 6/55; L 6/64; 769 6/65 | | 8.67 |
| 96 | L; 767 6/55; L 6/64; 769 6/65 | | 7.67 |
| 97 | L; 801 6/57; 803 6/64 | | 7.67 |
| 98 | L; 801 6/57; L 6/63; 73 6/65 | | 7.67 |
| 99 | L; 86 7/61; 812 6/64; L 6/65 | | 8.67 |
| 100 | L; 858 6/62 | | 7.67 |
| 101 | L; 80 6/62 | | 8.67 |

Tavern car No. S7897 'At the Sign of the Three Plovers' at Clapham Junction, 21st July, 1951; it was working with Restaurant Saloon No. S7834.

*H.C. Casserley*

Tavern car S7894 'Dolphin' working on the Eastern Region; Up 'Master Cutler' service near Chorley Wood on 23 July, 1949.

*H.C. Casserley*

The interior of third-class dining saloon of Tavern trailer before rebuilding; notice the lack of a view of the scenery, just sliding ventilators high up.

The restoration of Composite No. 5768 at Horsted Keynes during May 1976. *D. Gould*

No. 5768 at Horsted Keynes working on the Bluebell Railway on 20 May, 1978

*D. Gould*

Third Brake No. 2515, built in April 1951 and originally in Set 857, shown here at Sheffield Park on 14th April, 1979, after restoration in February 1977.

D. Gould

Birmingham RC&W Co. built Third Brake No. 4279 of January 1949 (Set 820), here shown as restored by the Bluebell Railway in April 1979; at Sheffield Park, 25th August, 1980.

D. Gould

A corridor view of Third Brake No. 2515, shortly after its February 1977 restoration by
the Bluebell Railway.

*D. Gould*

The saloon of Third Brake No. 2515 after its restoration in 1977 by the Bluebell Railway.                    *D. Gould*

|      |                                  | Wdn.  |
|------|----------------------------------|-------|
| 102  | L; 80 7/61                       | 12.67 |
| 103  | L; 80 6/61                       | 8.67  |
| 104  | L; 825 6/63; 808 6/64            | 9.66  |
| 105  | L; 873 11/60; L 6/63; 72 6/65    | 10.67 |
| 106  | L; 826 11/59; 809 6/64           | 7.67  |
| 107  | L; 826 11/59; 809 6/64           | 7.67  |
| 108  | L; 827 11/59; 810 6/64; L 6/65   | 12.66 |
| 109  | L; 827 11/59; 810 6/64; L 6/65   | 10.67 |
| 110  | L; 828 11/59; 811 6/64; L 6/65   | 9.67  |
| 111  | L; 828 11/59; 811 6/64; L 6/65   | 8.67  |
| 112  | L; 829 11/59; 80 6/64; 68 6/65   | 6.67  |
| 113  | L; 829 11/59; 812 6/64; L 6/65   | 7.67  |
| 114  | L; 830 11/59                     | 11.67 |
| 115  | L; 830 11/59                     | 9.67  |
| 116  | L; 831 11/59                     | 9.67  |
| 117  | L; 831 11/59                     | 7.67  |
| 118  | L; 832 11/59                     | 9.65  |
| 119  | L; 832 11/59                     | 9.64  |
| 120  | L; 833 11/59                     | 7.67  |
| 121  | L; 833 11/59                     | 7.67  |
| 122  | L; 802 6/57; L 6/63; 803 6/64    | 7.67  |

|      |                                      |     | Wdn.  |
|------|--------------------------------------|-----|-------|
| 123  | L; 834, 6/53                         |     | 12.67 |
| 124  | L; 834 6/53                          |     | 7.67  |
| 125  | L; 835 6/53                          |     | 7.67  |
| 126  | L; 835 6/53                          |     | 8.67  |
| 127  | L; 836 6/53                          |     | 5.64  |
| 128  | L; 836 6/53                          |     | 5.67  |
| 129  | L; 837 6/53                          |     | 9.67  |
| 130  | L; 837 6/53                          |     | 12.67 |
| 1727 | ex Compo 9/64                        | 981 | 8.67  |
| 1728 | ex Compo 9/64                        | 964 | 8.66  |
| 1729 | ex Compo 8/64                        | 980 | 8.67  |
| 1730 | ex Compo 4/64                        | 984 | 8.67  |
| 1932 | L; 86 6/61; 823 6/63; 967 6/64       |     | 8.67  |
| 1933 | L; 86 6/61; 967 6/64                 |     | 12.67 |
| 1934 | L; 400 9/51; L 11/59; 86 6/61; 967 6/64 | | 5.68 |
| 1935 | L; 804 6/59                          |     | 9.67  |
| 1936 | L; 804 6/59                          |     | 8.67  |

## Open Thirds

|      |                                      |         | Wdn.  |
|------|--------------------------------------|---------|-------|
| 1451 | 290; L 6/65                          |         | 10.68 |
| 1452 | 291; 770 6/64                        |         | 10.68 |
| 1453 | 292; 212 6/64                        |         | 11.68 |
| 1454 | 293; 885 6/64                        |         | 6.68  |
| 1455 | 294                                  |         | 9.67  |
| 1456 | 295; 212 6/64                        |         | 8.66  |
| 1457 | 296; 212 6/64                        |         | 9.66  |
| 1458 | 297                                  |         | 8.66  |
| 1459 | 298                                  |         | 12.66 |
| 1460 | 299; L 6/63                          |         | 7.67  |
| 1461 | 300; L 6/65                          |         | 7.67  |
| 1462 | L; 350 6/53; L 6/54                  |         | 9.67  |
| 1463 | 354 6/51; L 9/54, 770 6/65           |         | 10.68 |
| 1464 | L                                    |         | 11.68 |
| 1465 | L; 770 6/63                          |         | 5.67  |
| 1466 | L                                    | To ScR  | 10.65 |
| 1467 | 351 6/51; L 6/54                     | To ER   | 9.65  |
| 1468 | 351; L 6/54; 212 6/64               |         | 9.67  |
| 1469 | 352 6/51; L 6/54                     | To ER   | 9.65  |
| 1470 | L; 350 6/53; L 6/54                  | To ER   | 9.65  |
| 1471 | L                                    | To ScR  | 10.65 |
| 1472 | 354 6/51; L 9/54                     | To ER   | 9.65  |
| 1473 | L                                    |         | 11.67 |
| 1474 | L                                    | To ER   | 9.65  |
| 1475 | 351 6/51; L 6/54                     |         | 10.68 |
| 1476 | 350 6/51; L 6/53; 212 6/64           |         | 11.67 |
| 1477 | 350 6/51; L 6/53, 80 6/59; L 6/62    |         | 7.67  |
| 1478 | 350 6/51; L 6/53                     |         | 10.67 |
| 1479 | 350 6/51; L 6/53; 80 6/59, L 6/62    | To ScR  | 1.66  |
| 1480 | 350 6/51; L 6/53                     | To ER   | 8.65  |

|      |                                      |         | Wdn.  |
|------|--------------------------------------|---------|-------|
| 1481 | 353 6/51; L 6/54; 300 6/65           |         | 8.68  |
| 1482 | 350 6/53; L 6/54; 86 6/59; L 6/62    | To ScR  | 1.66  |
| 1483 | L                                    |         | 10.68 |
| 1484 | L                                    | To ScR  | 12.65 |
| 1485 | 352 6/51; L 6/54                     |         | 10.67 |
| 1486 | 353 6/51; L 6/54; 770 6/64           | To ER   | 8.65  |
| 1487 | L; 86 6/59; L 6/62                   |         | 1.65  |
| 1488 | L                                    |         | 11.68 |
| 1489 | L                                    | To ScR  | 2.66  |
| 1490 | L                                    | To ER   | 1.66  |
| 1491 | 352 6/51; L 6/54; 770 6/64           | To ER   | 12.65 |
| 1492 | L                                    |         | 10.68 |
| 1493 | L                                    |         | 7.67  |
| 1494 | L                                    |         | 8.67  |
| 1495 | 351 6/51; L 6/54                     | To ScR  | 4.66  |
| 1496 | 353 6/51; L 6/54; 770 6/64           |         | 10.68 |
| 1497 | L                                    |         | 10.67 |
| 1498 | 352 6/51; L 6/54                     | To ScR  | 4.66  |
| 1499 | 353 6/51; L 6/54                     | To ER   | 1.66  |
| 1500 | L; 350 6/53; L 6/54; 212 6/64        | To ScR  | 1.66  |
| 1501 | 352 6/51; L 6/54; 770 6/64           |         | 8.67  |
| 1502 | 352 6/51; L 6/54                     | To ScR  | 10.65 |
| 1503 | 354 6/51; L 9/54; 770 6/64           | To ScR  | 9.65  |
| 1504 | 354 6/51; L 9/54; 212 6/64           |         | 11.68 |
| 1505 | L; 350 6/53; L 6/54                  | To ER   | 9.65  |
| 1506 | L                                    |         | 8.67  |

## Corridor Third Brakes

| No. | | | Wdn. |
|---|---|---|---|
| 2501 | 850 | 6/51 | 10.66 |
| 2502 | 850 | 6/51 | 10.66 |
| 2503 | 851 | 6/51 | 12.65 |
| 2504 | 851 | 6/51 | 12.65 |
| 2505 | 852 | 6/51 | 9.66 |
| 2506 | 852 | 6/51 | 7.67 |
| 2507 | 853 | 6/51 | 8.67 |
| 2508 | 853 | 6/51 | 7.67 |
| 2509 | 854 | 6/51 | 3.67 |
| 2510 | 854 | 6/51 | 7.67 |
| 2511 | 855 | 6/51 | 8.67 |
| 2512 | 855 | 6/51 | 8.67 |
| 2513 | 856 | 6/51 | 4.64 |
| 2514 | 856 | 6/51 | 4.64 |
| 2515 | 857 | 6/51 | 9.66 |
| 2516 | 857 | 6/51 | 7.66 |
| 2517 | 858 | 6/51 | 8.67 |
| 2518 | 858 | 6/51 | 8.67 |
| 2519 | 859 | 6/51 | 4.67 |
| 2520 | 859 | 6/51 | 12.67 |
| 2521 | 860 | 6/51 | 11.65 |
| 2522 | 860 | 6/51 | 11.65 |
| 2523 | 861 | 6/51 | 1.65 |
| 2524 | 861 | 6/51 | 10.66 |
| 2525 | 862 | 6/51 | 10.67 |
| 2526 | 862 | 6/51 | 3.67 |
| 2527 | 863 | 6/51 | 5.66 |
| 2528 | 863 | 6/51 | 5.66 |
| 2529 | 864 | 6/51 | |
| | | L 6/64 | 7.67 |
| 2530 | 864 | | |
| | | L 6/64 | 8.67 |
| 2531 | 865 | 6/51 | 12.65 |
| 2532 | 865 | 6/51 | 4.64 |
| 2841 | 963 | | 12.63 |
| 2842 | 963 | | 12.63 |
| 2843 | 964 | | 11.66 |
| 2844 | 964 | | 8.67 |
| 2845 | 965 | | 12.63 |
| 2846 | 965 | | 12.63 |
| 2847 | 966 | | 12.63 |
| 2848 | 966 | | 12.63 |
| 2849 | 967 | | 10.67 |
| 2850 | 967 | | 11.65 |
| 2851 | 968 | | 7.67 |
| 2852 | 968 | | 12.67 |
| 2853 | 969 | | 12.63 |
| 2854 | 969 | | 12.63 |
| 2855 | 970 | | 12.63 |
| 2856 | 970 | | 12.63 |
| 2857 | 971 | | 12.63 |
| 2858 | 971 | | 12.63 |
| 2859 | 972 | | 12.63 |
| 2860 | 972 | | 12.63 |
| 2861 | 973; 984 6/64 | | 8.67 |
| 2862 | 973 | | 12.63 |

| No. | | | Wdn. |
|---|---|---|---|
| 2863 | 974 | | 12.63 |
| 2864 | 974 | | 12.63 |
| 2865 | 975 | | 12.63 |
| 2866 | 975 | | 12.63 |
| 2867 | 976 | | 7.67 |
| 2868 | 976 | | 9.67 |
| 2869 | 977 | | 12.63 |
| 2870 | 977 | | 12.63 |
| 2871 | 978 | | 12.63 |
| 2872 | 978 | | 12.63 |
| 2873 | 979 | | 12.63 |
| 2874 | 979 | | 12.63 |
| 2875 | 980 | | 7.67 |
| 2876 | 980 | | 7.66 |
| 2877 | 981 | | 8.67 |
| 2878 | 981 | | 7.67 |
| 2879 | 982 | | 12.63 |
| 2880 | 982 | | 12.63 |
| 2881 | 983 | | 12.63 |
| 2882 | 983 | | 12.63 |
| 2883 | 984 | | 12.63 |
| 2884 | 984 | | 10.67 |
| 3943 | L; 766 6/61; | | |
| | L 9/61; 430 6/63 | | 5.64 |
| 3944 | L; 804 6/59 | | 10.67 |
| 3945 | L; 804 6/59 | | 7.67 |
| 3946 | 264 6/50 | | 12.65 |
| 3947 | 264 6/50 | | 12.65 |
| 3948 | 267 6/50; L 6/59; | | |
| | 766 6/61; | | |
| | 803 11/61 | | 7.67 |
| 3949 | 267 6/50; L 6/59; | | |
| | 237 7/61 | | 12.65 |
| 3950 | 767 6/50 | | 5.66 |
| 3951 | 767 6/50 | | 5.66 |
| 3952 | 768 6/50 | | 9.65 |
| 3953 | 768 6/50 | | 5.66 |
| 3954 | 769 6/50 | | 1.66 |
| 3955 | 769 6/50 | | 12.65 |
| 3956 | 266 6/50; | | |
| | 86 6/65 | | 7.66 |
| 3957 | 266 6/50; | | |
| | 861 6/65 | | 8.67 |
| 3958 | L; 468 6/61 | | 12.65 |
| 3959 | 265 6/50; L 6/59; | | |
| | 468 6/61 | | 12.67 |
| 3960 | 265 6/50; L6/59; | | |
| | 803 11/61 | | 8.67 |
| 3961 | L; 237 6/61 | | 7.64 |
| 3962 | L; 430 6/63; | | |
| | L 6/64 | | 8.65 |
| 3971 | 830 | 6/50 | 5.66 |
| 3972 | 830 | 6/50 | 10.66 |
| 3973 | 831 | 6/50 | 11.66 |
| 3974 | 831 | 6/50 | 9.66 |
| 3975 | 832 | 6/50 | 11.67 |

| No. | | | Wdn. |
|---|---|---|---|
| 3976 | 832 | 6/50 | 7.67 |
| 3977 | 833 | 6/50 | 11.67 |
| 3978 | 833 | 6/50 | 2.66 |
| 3979 | 834 | 6/50 | 10.66 |
| 3980 | 834 | 6/50 | 10.66 |
| 3981 | 835 | 6/50 | 7.67 |
| 3982 | 835 | 6/50 | 10.67 |
| 3983 | 836 | 6/50 | 7.67 |
| 3984 | 836 | 6/50 | 3.66 |
| 3985 | 837 | 6/50 | 10.66 |
| 3986 | 837 | 6/50 | 4.66 |
| 3987 | 838 | 6/50 | 10.66 |
| 3988 | 838 | 6/50 | 9.66 |
| 3989 | 839 | 6/50 | 5.66 |
| 3990 | 839 | 6/50 | 5.66 |
| 3991 | 840 | 6/50 | 10.67 |
| 3992 | 840 | 6/50 | 9.67 |
| 3993 | 841 | 6/50 | 12.66 |
| 3994 | 841 | 6/50 | 9.67 |
| 3995 | 842 | 6/50 | 9.67 |
| 3996 | 842 | 6/50 | 8.67 |
| 3997 | 843 | 6/50 | 7.67 |
| 3998 | 843 | | 11.67 |
| 3999 | 844 | 6/50 | 10.66 |
| 4000 | 844 | 6/50 | 7.67 |
| 4001 | 845 | 6/50 | 1.66 |
| 4002 | 845 | 6/50 | 1.66 |
| 4003 | 846 | 6/50 | 8.67 |
| 4004 | 846 | 6/50 | 1.68 |
| 4005 | 847 | 6/50 | 7.67 |
| 4006 | 847 | 6/50 | 8.67 |
| 4007 | 848 | 6/50 | 6.66 |
| 4008 | 848 | 6/50 | 2.66 |
| 4009 | 849 | 6/50 | 8.67 |
| 4010 | 849 | 6/50 | 8.67 |
| 4011 | 80 | 5/49 | 7.67 |
| 4012 | 80 | 5/49 | 10.66 |
| 4013 | 81 | 5/49 | 5.64 |
| 4014 | 81 | 5/49 | 5.64 |
| 4015 | 82 | 5/49 | 5.66 |
| 4016 | 82 | 5/49 | 6.66 |
| 4017 | 83 | 5/49 | 8.67 |
| 4018 | 83 | 5/49 | 7.67 |
| 4019 | 84 | 5/49 | 5.64 |
| 4020 | 84 | 5/49 | 5.64 |
| 4021 | 85 | 5/49 | 10.66 |
| 4022 | 85 | 5/49 | 5.66 |
| 4023 | 86 | 5/49 | 1.65 |
| 4024 | 86 | 5/49 | 6.66 |
| 4025 | 87 | 5/49 | 2.65 |
| 4026 | 87 | 5/49 | 2.65 |
| 4027 | 88 | 5/49 | 10.66 |
| 4028 | 88 | 5/49 | 10.66 |
| 4029 | 89 | 5/49 | 5.64 |
| 4030 | 89 | 5/49 | 5.64 |
| 4031 | 90 | 5/49 | 10.66 |

| No. | | | Wdn. |
|---|---|---|---|
| 4032 | 90 | 5/49 | 12.66 |
| 4033 | 91 | 5/49 | 2/65 |
| 4034 | 91 | 5/49 | 2.65 |
| 4035 | 92 | 5/49 | 1.65 |
| 4036 | 92 | 5/49 | 1.65 |
| 4037 | 93 | 5/49 | 6.64 |
| 4038 | 93 | 5/49 | 6.64 |
| 4039 | 94 | 5/49 | 7.66 |
| 4040 | 94 | 5/49 | 7.66 |
| 4209 | 795 Accident damage Eastbourne 17.4.58 | | |
| 4210 | 795; 821 6/59; 433 6/60; L 6/62; 156 6/64 To WR | | 10.64 |
| 4211 | 796 | To WR | 2.65 |
| 4212 | 796 | | 1.65 |
| 4213 | 797 | To WR | 10.64 |
| 4214 | 797 | To WR | 10.64 |
| 4215 | 798 | To WR | 1.65 |
| 4216 | 798 | To WR | 1.65 |
| 4217 | 799 | To WR | c. /67 |
| 4218 | 799 | To WR | c. /67 |
| 4219 | 800 | To WR | 1.65 |
| 4220 | 800 | To WR | 1.65 |
| 4221 | 801 | To WR | 11.64 |
| 4222 | 801 | To WR | 11.64 |
| 4223 | 802 | To WR | 11.64 |
| 4224 | 802 | To WR | 11.64 |
| 4225 | 803 473 6/54; 211 6/55; 897 6/58; L 6/64 To WR | | 11.64 |
| 4226 | 803; 473 6/54; 211 6/55; 897 6/58; L 6/64. To WR | | 2.65 |
| 4227 | 804; 474 6/54 To WR | | 1.65 |
| 4228 | 804; 474 6/54 To WR | | 1.65 |
| 4229 | 805 | | 7.67 |
| 4230 | 805 | | 4.64 |
| 4251 | 806; L 6/64 | | 4.66 |
| 4252 | 806; L 6/64 | | 10.67 |
| 4253 | 807; | | 5.66 |
| 4254 | 807 | | 5.66 |
| 4255 | 808 | | 10.66 |
| 4256 | 808 | | 9.66 |
| 4257 | 809 | | 8.66 |
| 4258 | 809 | | 9.67 |
| 4259 | 810; L 6/65 | | 8.67 |
| 4260 | 810; L 6/65 | | 7.67 |
| 4261 | 811 | | 5.65 |
| 4262 | 811 | | 5.65 |
| 4263 | 812; L 6/65 | | 5.68 |
| 4264 | 812; L 6/65 | | 8.67 |
| 4265 | 813; L 6/65 | | 5.66 |

| No. | | | Wdn. |
|---|---|---|---|
| 4266 | 813; L 6/65 | | 9.67 |
| 4267 | 814; L 6/65 | | 9.67 |
| 4268 | 814; L 6/65 | | 12.66 |
| 4269 | 815 | | 8.67 |
| 4270 | 815 | | 6.66 |
| 4271 | 816 | | 12.67 |
| 4272 | 816 | | 7.67 |
| 4273 | 817 | | 12.65 |
| 4274 | 817 | | 9.67 |
| 4275 | 818 | | 9.66 |
| 4276 | 818 | | 7.66 |
| 4277 | 819 | | 10.66 |
| 4278 | 819 | | 8.66 |
| 4279 | 820 | | 4.66 |
| 4280 | 820 | | 8.67 |
| 4281 | 821 | | 3.56 |
| 4282 | 821; 76 6/60; To WR | | 3.65 |
| 4283 | 822 | | 5.66 |
| 4284 | 822 | | 5.66 |
| 4285 | 823 | | 5.64 |
| 4286 | 823 | | 5.64 |
| 4287 | 824 | | 6.66 |
| 4288 | 824 | | 6.66 |
| 4289 | 825 | | 2.65 |
| 4290 | 825 | | 2.65 |
| 4291 | 826 | | 7.67 |
| 4292 | 826 | | 7.67 |
| 4293 | 827 | | 1.65 |
| 4294 | 827 | | 1.65 |
| 4295 | 828 | | 9.66 |
| 4296 | 828 | | 9.66 |
| 4297 | 829 | | 4.64 |
| 4298 | 829 | | 4.64 |
| 4301 | 770 | | 12/67 |
| 4302 | 770 | | 5.67 |
| 4303 | 771 | | 11.66 |
| 4304 | 771 | | 10.66 |
| 4305 | 772 | | 4.64 |
| 4306 | 772 | | 4.64 |
| 4307 | 773 | To WR | 11.64 |
| 4308 | 773 | To WR | 11.64 |
| 4309 | 774 | To WR | 11.64 |
| 4310 | 774; L 6/65 | | 8.67 |
| 4311 | 775 | To WR | 1.65 |
| 4312 | 775 | To WR | 1.65 |
| 4313 | 776 | | 7.67 |
| 4314 | 776 | | 5.67 |
| 4315 | 777 | | 8.67 |
| 4316 | 777 | | 9.67 |
| 4317 | 778 | To WR | 1.65 |
| 4318 | 778 | To WR | 1.65 |
| 4319 | 779 | To WR | 11.64 |
| 4320 | 779 | To WR | 11.64 |
| 4321 | 780 | | 11.67 |
| 4322 | 780 | | 9.67 |
| 4323 | 781 | | 8.67 |
| 4324 | 781 | | 12.67 |
| 4325 | 782 | | 5.64 |
| 4326 | 782 | | 5.64 |

| No. | | | Wdn. |
|---|---|---|---|
| 4327 | 783 | To WR | 11.64 |
| 4328 | 783 | To WR | 11.64 |
| 4329 | 784 | To WR | 10.64 |
| 4330 | 784 | To WR | 10.64 |
| 4331 | 785 | To WR | 1.65 |
| 4332 | 785 | To WR | 1.65 |
| 4333 | 786 | | 7.66 |
| 4334 | 786 | | 10.67 |
| 4335 | 787 | | 11.67 |
| 4336 | 787 | | 8.67 |
| 4337 | 788 | | 11.66 |
| 4338 | 788 | | 11.66 |
| 4339 | 789 | To WR | 11.64 |
| 4340 | 789 | To WR | 11.64 |
| 4341 | 790 | | 9.67 |
| 4342 | 790 | | 9.67 |
| 4343 | 791; L 6/65 | | 9.66 |
| 4344 | 791; L 6/65 | | 12.65 |
| 4345 | 792 | | 8.67 |
| 4346 | 792 | | 8.67 |
| 4347 | 793 | | 8.67 |
| 4348 | 793 | | 7.67 |
| 4349 | 290; 212 6/65 | | 12.67 |
| 4350 | 290; 212 6/65 | | 12.65 |
| 4351 | 291; 805 6/64 | | 9.66 |
| 4352 | 291; 865 6/64 | | 9.66 |
| 4353 | 292; 212 6/64; 299 6/65 | | 8.67 |
| 4354 | 292; 212 6/64; To WR | | 2.65 |
| 4355 | 293 | | 8.65 |
| 4356 | 293 | | 10.66 |
| 4357 | 294 | | 9.66 |
| 4358 | 294 | | 12.67 |
| 4359 | 295 | | 5.64 |
| 4360 | 295 | | 5.64 |
| 4361 | 296; 237 6/64 | | 11.66 |
| 4362 | 296 | | 4.64 |
| 4363 | 297 | | 9.67 |
| 4364 | 297 | | 9.67 |
| 4365 | 298; L 6/65 | | 5.66 |
| 4366 | 298; L 6/65 | | 5.66 |
| 4367 | 299; L 6/65 | | 7.66 |
| 4368 | 299; 952 6/65 | | 8.67 |
| 4369 | 300; L 6/65 | | 7.66 |
| 4370 | 300; L 6/65 | | 7.67 |
| 4371 | 63; 701 6/65 | | 7.67 |
| 4372 | 64; 156 6/65 | | 9.66 |
| 4373 | 65 | | 5.64 |
| 4374 | 66 | | 11.67 |
| 4375 | 67 | | 5.64 |
| 4376 | 68; 702 6/65 | | 12.67 |
| 4377 | 69; 702 6/65 | | 7.67 |
| 4378 | 70; 703 6/65 | | 8.67 |
| 4379 | 71 | | 1.65 |
| 4380 | 72; 703 6/65 | | 12.67 |
| 4381 | 73; 701 6/65 | | 11.67 |
| 4382 | 74 | | 6.64 |
| 4383 | 75 | | 4.65 |

## Corridor Composites

| No. | Details | Wdn. |
|---|---|---|
| 5709 | 963 | 12.63 |
| 5710 | 964 | 8.67 |
| 5711 | 965 | 12.63 |
| 5712 | 966 | 12.63 |
| 5713 | 967 | 12.63 |
| 5714 | 968 | 8.67 |
| 5715 | 969 | 12.63 |
| 5716 | 970 | 12.63 |
| 5717 | 971 | 12.63 |
| 5718 | 972 | 12.63 |
| 5719 | 973; 967 6/64 | 7.67 |
| 5720 | 974 | 12.63 |
| 5721 | 975 | 12.63 |
| 5722 | 976 | 1.68 |
| 5723 | 977 | 12.63 |
| 5724 | 978 | 12.63 |
| 5725 | 979 | 12.63 |
| 5726 | 980 | 9.66 |
| 5727 | Re-No. 1727 | 9.64 |
| 5728 | Re-No. 1728 | 9.64 |
| 5729 | Re-No. 1729 | 8.64 |
| 5730 | Re-No. 1730 (As Compos, were in sets 981-4) | 4.64 |
| 5740 | 290; L 6/64; 523 6/65 | 10.68 |
| 5741 | 291; 769 6/64 | 9.67 |
| 5742 | 292; L 6/64 | 11.64 |
| 5743 | 293 | 7.67 |
| 5744 | 294 | 2.65 |
| 5745 | 295 | 5.64 |
| 5746 | 296 | 5.64 |
| 5747 | 297 | 8.67 |
| 5748 | 298 | 7.67 |
| 5749 | 299; L 6/65 | 9.67 |
| 5750 | 300 | 9.67 |
| 5751 | 770; 976 6/64 | 7.67 |
| 5752 | 771 | 8.67 |
| 5753 | 772 | 4.64 |
| 5754 | 773 | 11.64 |
| 5755 | 774 | 11.64 |
| 5756 | 775 | 10.64 |
| 5757 | 776 | 1.68 |
| 5758 | 777 | 12.67 |
| 5759 | 778 | 11.64 |
| 5760 | 779 | 11.64 |
| 5761 | 780 | 12.68 |
| 5762 | 781 | 9.67 |
| 5763 | 782 | 5.64 |
| 5764 | 783 | 11.64 |
| 5765 | 784 | 11.64 |
| 5766 | 785 | 11.64 |

| No. | Details | Wdn. |
|---|---|---|
| 5767 | 786 | 8.67 |
| 5768 | 787 | 10.68 |
| 5769 | 788 | 8.67 |
| 5770 | 789 | 10.64 |
| 5771 | 790 | 9.67 |
| 5772 | 791 | 2.65 |
| 5773 | 792 | 8.67 |
| 5774 | 793 | 7.67 |
| 5775 | 795; L 6/59; 268 11/59;443 6/62; L 6/64 | 7.67 |
| 5776 | 796 | 11.64 |
| 5777 | 797 | 11.64 |
| 5778 | 798 | 11.64 |
| 5779 | 799 | 8.67 |
| 5780 | 800 | 10.64 |
| 5781 | 801; L 6/57 | 1.67 |
| 5782 | 802; L 6/57 | 9.66 |
| 5783 | 803; 474 6/54 | 11.64 |
| 5784 | 804; 474 6/54 | 11.64 |
| 5785 | 805; 244 6/57; 269 6/58; 80 6/62 | 8.67 |
| 5786 | 806; L 6/64 | 11.64 |
| 5787 | 807 | 9.66 |
| 5788 | 808 | 12.66 |
| 5789 | 809 | 1.68 |
| 5790 | 810; L 6/65 | 12.65 |
| 5791 | 811 | 3.65 |
| 5792 | 812; L 6/65 | 7.67 |
| 5793 | 813; L 6/65 | 12.65 |
| 5794 | 814 | 12.64 |
| 5795 | 815 | 9.66 |
| 5796 | 816 | 8.67 |
| 5797 | 817 | 12.65 |
| 5798 | 818 | 10.66 |
| 5799 | L; 434 11/59; 238 6/60; L 4/61; 242 9/61; 443 6/62; 769 6/64 | 2.66 |
| 5800 | L; 434 11/59; 235 6/60; L 4/61; 250 9/61; 768 6/63 | 7.67 |
| 5801 | L; 469 6/54; L 6/55; 201 11/59; 436 6/60; L 6/63 | 1.66 |
| 5802 | L; 469 6/54; L 6/55; 201 11/59; 207 6/60; 432 6/62; 952 6/64 | 9.67 |
| 5803 | L; 400 9/51; 206 11/59; 249 6/62; L 6/63; 527 6/64; 526 6/65 | 5.66 |
| 5804 | L; 206 11/59; 249 6/62; 432 6/63; 529 6/64 | 6.67 |

| No. | Details | | Wdn. |
|---|---|---|---|
| 5805 | L; 442 6/60; L 9/61;428 6/62; L 6/64 | | 12.65 |
| 5806 | L; 436 6/60; 978 6/63 | | 5.64 |
| 5807 | L; 442 6/60; L 9/61; 428 6/62; L 6/64; 838 6/65 | | 8.67 |
| 5808 | L; 239 11/59; 982 6/62; L 6/64; 294 6/65 | | 5.67 |
| 5809 | L; 350 6/59; L 6/65 | | 8.67 |
| 5810 | L; 351 6/59; L 6/65 | | 7.67 |
| 5811 | L; 352 6/59; L 6/65 | | 2.66 |
| 5812 | 819 | | 10.67 |
| 5813 | 820 | | 9.66 |
| 5814 | 821; L 6/60; 250 6.62; 769 6/63 | | 5.64 |
| 5815 | 822 | | 9.66 |
| 5816 | 823 | | 5.64 |
| 5817 | 824 | | 7.67 |
| 5818 | 825 | | 2.65 |
| 5819 | 826 | | 8.67 |
| 5820 | 827 | | 1.65 |
| 5821 | 828 | | 7.67 |
| 5822 | 829 | | 4.64 |
| 5823 | 80 | 5/49 | 10.67 |
| 5824 | 81 | 5/49 | 5.64 |
| 5825 | 82 | 5/49 | 10.66 |
| 5826 | 83 | 5/49 | 9.67 |
| 5827 | 84 | 5/49 | 5.64 |
| 5828 | 85 | 5/49 | 10.66 |
| 5829 | 86 | 5/49 | 10.66 |
| 5830 | 87 | 5/49 | 2.65 |
| 5831 | 88 | 5/49 | 4.67 |
| 5832 | 89 | 5/49 | 5.64 |
| 5833 | 90 | 5/49 | 7.67 |
| 5834 | 91 | 5/49 | 2.65 |
| 5835 | 92 | 5/49 | 1.65 |
| 5836 | 93 | 5/49 | 6.64 |
| 5837 | 94 | 5/49 | 9.66 |
| 5848 | 830 | 6/50 | 9.67 |
| 5849 | 831 | 6/50 | 8.67 |
| 5850 | 832 | 6/50 | 8.67 |
| 5851 | 833 | 6/50 | 4.67 |
| 5852 | 834 | 6/50 | 7.67 |
| 5853 | 835 | 6/50 | 12.65 |
| 5854 | 836 | 6/50 | 8.67 |

| | | | Wdn. | | | Wdn. | | | Wdn. |
|---|---|---|---|---|---|---|---|---|---|
| 5855 | 837 | 6/50 | 8.67 | 5878 | 767 6/50; 959 6/62; | | 5898 | L Accident damage | |
| 5856 | 838 | 6/50 | 2.65 | | 802 6/64 | 11.64 | | | 4.53 |
| 5857 | 839 | 6/50 | 9.68 | 5879 | 769 6/50 | 6/64 | 5899 | L; 875 6/53; | |
| 5858 | 840 | 6/50 | 1.68 | 5880 | 768 6/50 | 11.64 | | L 6/62; 559 6/64 | 9.66 |
| 5859 | 841 | 6/50 | 7.67 | 5881 | 264 6/50 | 12.65 | 5900 | L; 961 6/62; 973 | |
| 5860 | 842 | 6/50 | 10.68 | 5882 | 264 6/50; L 6/64 | 6.67 | | 6/63; 967 6/64 | 7.67 |
| 5861 | 843 | 6/50 | 10.67 | 5883 | 263 6/50; L 6/55; | | 5901 | L | 9.67 |
| 5862 | 844 | 6/50 | 9.66 | | 804 6/57 | 7.67 | 5902 | L | 8.67 |
| 5863 | 845 | 6/50 | 1.66 | 5884 | 263 6/50; L 6/55; 80 | | 5903 | L; 874 6/53; | |
| 5864 | 846 | 6/50 | 8.67 | | 6/59; 981 6/64 | 8.67 | | L 6/65 | 8.67 |
| 5865 | 847 | 6/50 | 8.67 | 5885 | 263 6/50; L 6/55; | | 5904 | L; 803 6/57 | 8.67 |
| 5866 | 848 | 6/50 | 7.67 | | 444 6/60; 271 6/62; | | 5905 | L | 3.67 |
| 5867 | 849 | 6/50 | 2.66 | | 984 6/64 | 7.67 | 5906 | L; 556 6/63 | 9.66 |
| 5868 | 265 6/50; 263 6/59; | | | 5886 | L; 86 6/59; | | 5907 | L; 265 6/55; L 6/59; | |
| | L 11/59; 981 6/62 | 1.68 | | | L 6/64 | 9.66 | | 433 6/62; | |
| 5869 | 265 6/50; 263 6/59; | | | 5887 | L; 802 6/55; L 6/57; | | | 964 6/64 | 1.68 |
| | L 11/59; 983 6/62; | | | | 885 6/65 | 8.67 | 5908 | 850 | 6/51 | 10.66 |
| | L 6/64 | 10.67 | | 5888 | L; 444 6/60; | | 5909 | 851 | 6/51 | 12.65 |
| 5870 | 265 6/50; L 6/59; | | | | 803 6/63 | 8.67 | 5910 | 852 | 6/51 | 8.67 |
| | 956 6/62; L 6/64; | | | 5889 | L; 767 6/64 | 11.66 | 5911 | 853 | 6/51 | 9.66 |
| | 570 6/65 | 8.67 | | 5890 | L; 904 6/59; | | 5912 | 854 | 6/51 | 9.67 |
| 5871 | 267 6/50; L 6/59; | | | | 878 6/64 | 7.67 | 5913 | 855 | 6/51 | 9.67 |
| | 955 6/62 | 5.64 | | 5891 | L; 904 6/59; | | 5914 | 856 | 6/51 | 4.64 |
| 5872 | 267 6/50; L 6/59; | | | | 801 6/64 | 11.64 | 5915 | 857 | 6/51 | 7.67 |
| | 984 6/62 | 9.67 | | 5892 | L 6/50; 873 6/55; | | 5916 | 858 | 6/51 | |
| 5873 | 267 6/50; L 6/59; | | | | 766 6/61; L 9/61; | | | L 6/64; 66 6/65 | 8.67 |
| | 952 6/62 | 5.64 | | | 536 6/63 | 8.67 | 5917 | 859 | 6/51 | 7.67 |
| 5874 | 267 6/50; L 6/59; | | | 5893 | L; 557 6/63 | 10.67 | 5918 | 860 | 6/51 | 11.65 |
| | 980 6/62 | 10.67 | | 5894 | L; 207 6/60; 432 | | 5919 | 861 | 6/51 | 8.67 |
| 5875 | 266 6/50 | 11.64 | | | 6/62; 804 6/64 | 7.67 | 5920 | 862 | 6/51 | 10.67 |
| 5876 | 266 6/50; | | | 5895 | L; 858 6/62; | | 5921 | 863 | 6/51 | 9.66 |
| | 979 6/63 | 5.64 | | | L 6/65 | 10.67 | 5922 | 864 | 6/51 | |
| 5877 | L; 430 6/57; L 9/60; | | | 5896 | L; 433 6/62 | 5.64 | | 858 6/63 | 1.67 |
| | 271 6/62 | 6.64 | | 5897 | L; 960 6/62; | | 5923 | 865 | 6/51 | 12.65 |
| | | | | | 984 6/64 | 8.67 | | | |

## Corridor Brake Composites

| | | | Wdn. | | | | Wdn. | | | | Wdn. |
|---|---|---|---|---|---|---|---|---|---|---|---|
| 6700 | 63 | | 12.67 | 6718 | L | | 5.64 | 6736 | L | | 7.67 |
| 6701 | 64 | | 11.64 | 6719 | L | To WR | 12.62 | 6737 | L | | 11.64 |
| 6702 | 65 | | 6.64 | 6720 | L | | 7.64 | 6738 | L; 400 9/51; L | | |
| 6703 | 66 | | 8.67 | 6721 | L | | 1.65 | | 11/59 To WR | | 12.62 |
| 6704 | 67 | | 6.64 | 6722 | L | | 12.65 | 6739 | L | | 11.64 |
| 6705 | 68 | | 7.67 | 6723 | L | | 12.65 | 6740 | L | | 11.64 |
| 6706 | 69 | | 5.66 | 6724 | L | | 6.64 | 6741 | L | | 12.67 |
| 6707 | 70 | | 7.67 | 6725 | L | | 10.64 | 6742 | L | To WR | 11.64 |
| 6708 | 71 | | 11.64 | 6726 | L | To WR | 12.62 | 6743 | L | | 11.64 |
| 6709 | 72 | | 12.67 | 6727 | L | | 12.67 | 6744 | L | | 6.64 |
| 6710 | 73 | | 12.67 | 6728 | L; 400 9/51: | | | 6745 | L | | 8.64 |
| 6711 | 74 | | 5.64 | | L 11/59 | | 11.64 | 6746 | L | To WR | 11.64 |
| 6712 | 75 | | 11.64 | 6729 | L | | 12.67 | 6747 | L | | 9.65 |
| | | | | 6730 | L | | 5.64 | 6748 | L | | 11.64 |
| 6713 | L; 76 6/60 | | 11.64 | 6731 | L | | 5.64 | 6749 | L | | 9.64 |
| 6714 | L | To WR | 12.62 | 6732 | L | | 8.64 | 6750 | L | | 5.64 |
| 6715 | L | To WR | 12.62 | 6733 | L | | 11.64 | 6751 | L | | 11.64 |
| 6716 | L | To WR | 12.62 | 6734 | L | | 3.67 | 6752 | L | | 11.64 |
| 6717 | L | To WR | 12.62 | 6735 | L; 952 6/64 | | 12.67 | | | | |

## Corridor Firsts

| No. | Details | Wdn. | No. | Details | Wdn. | No. | Details | Wdn. |
|---|---|---|---|---|---|---|---|---|
| 7608 | L; 353 6/51; L 6/52; 353 6/57; L 6/63 | 5.64 | 7625 | L; 427 6/54; L 6/62 | 7.65 | 7644 | L; 235 6/55; L 6/57; 468 6/62 | 11.64 |
| 7609 | L; 352 6/51; 353 6/52 | 5.65 | 7626 | L | 6.65 | 7645 | L; 767 6/55; L 6/64 | 10.65 |
| 7610 | L; 350 6/51; L 6/53; 353 9/60 | 3.65 | 7627 | L; 351 6/51 | 2.65 | 7646 | L; 236 6/55; L 6/57; 897 6/60; L 6/63 | 9.65 |
| 7611 | L | 4.65 | 7628 | L | 6.65 | 7647 | L; 237 6/55; L 6/57; 804 6/62; 290 6/64 | 2.65 |
| 7612 | L | 3.65 | 7629 | L | 5.64 | 7648 | L; 473 6/54; L 6/59; 299 6/65 | 12.67 |
| 7613 | L; 355 6/51; L 6/52 | 11.64 | 7630 | L; 802 6/57; L 6/64 | 9.65 | 7677 | 290; 294 6/65 | 9.67 |
| 7614 | L; 355 6/51; L 6/52 | 11.64 | 7631 | L; 876 6/53; L 6/63 | 12.65 | 7678 | 291; L 6/64 | 2.65 |
| 7615 | L; 356 6/51; L 6/52; 354 6/57; L /63 | 7.65 | 7632 | L; 443 11/59; L 6/62; 237 6/64 | 11.65 | 7679 | 292; L 6/64 | 11.64 |
| 7616 | L; 356 6/51; L 6/52 | 1.68 | 7633 | L; 560 6/64 | 9.65 | 7680 | 293; L 6/64 | 2.65 |
| 7617 | L; 350 6/53 | 9.65 | 7634 | L; 803 /62; L/63 | 8.65 | 7681 | 294 | 3.65 |
| 7618 | L; 353 6/51 | 6.65 | 7635 | L; 801 6/57 | 5.64 | 7682 | 295 | 12.63 |
| 7619 | L; 352 6/52 | 3.65 | 7636 | L | 5.64 | 7683 | 296; L 6/64; 297 6/65 | 9.67 |
| 7620 | L; 354 6/51 | 3.65 | 7637 | L | 5.64 | 7684 | 297 | 11.64 |
| 7621 | L; 354 6/51 | 3.65 | 7638 | L | 5.64 | 7685 | 298 | 2.65 |
| 7622 | L; 805 6/57 | 10.64 | 7639 | L | 5.64 | 7686 | 299 | 1.65 |
| 7623 | L; 354 9/60 | 3.65 | 7640 | L; 237 6/61 | 5.64 | 7687 | 300 | 3.65 |
| 7624 | L | 8.65 | 7641 | L | 2.65 | | | |
| | | | 7642 | L | 11.64 | | | |
| | | | 7643 | L; 234 6/55; L 6/57 | 3.65 | | | |

| No. | Details | Wdn. | No. | Details | Wdn. | No. | Details | Wdn. |
|---|---|---|---|---|---|---|---|---|
| 7833 | L | 2.65 | 7836 | L | 9.67 | 7839 | L | 9.67 |
| 7834 | L | 2.65 | 7837 | L | 7.65 | 7840 | L | 2.65 |
| 7835 | L | 8.67 | 7838 | L | 9.67 | | | |

## Kitchen/Dining Thirds

| No. | Details | Wdn. | No. | Details | Wdn. | No. | Details | Wdn. |
|---|---|---|---|---|---|---|---|---|
| 7881 | 290; L 6/62 | 1.64 | 7887 | 296; L 6/62 | 1.64 | 7894 | L | 1.68 |
| 7882 | 291; L 6/62 | 1.64 | 7888 | 297; L 6/62 | 1.64 | 7895 | L | 1.67 |
| 7883 | 292; L 6/62 | 1.64 | 7889 | 298; L 6/62 | 6.65 | 7896 | L | 9.67 |
| 7884 | 293; L 6/62 | 1.64 | 7890 | 299; L 6/62 | 7.65 | 7897 | L | 12.66 |
| 7885 | 294; L 6/62 | 1.64 | 7891 | 300; L 6/62 | 7.65 | 7898 | L | 1.68 |
| 7886 | 295; L 6/62 | 1.64 | 7892 | L | 1.68 | 7899 | L | 1.68 |
| | | | 7893 | L | 1.67 | | | |

## Disposals of Coaches Transferred to Other BR Regions

### Eastern Region (Open Seconds)

|      | Wdn.  |      | Wdn.  |      | Wdn.  |
|------|-------|------|-------|------|-------|
| 1467 | 9.67  | 1474 | 4.66  | 1491 | ?     |
| 1469 | 4.69  | 1480 | ?     | 1499 | ?.68  |
| 1470 | 1.69  | 1486 | ?.66  | 1505 | ?     |
| 1472 | ?.66  | 1490 | 7.67  |      |       |

E 1469 S sold to Keighley & Worth Valley Railway, 1970.

### Scottish Region (Open Seconds)

|      | Wdn.  |      | Wdn.  |      | Wdn.  |
|------|-------|------|-------|------|-------|
| 1466 | 2.70  | 1484 | 6.68  | 1500 | 12.69 |
| 1471 | 9.67  | 1489 | 11.69 | 1502 | 2.70  |
| 1479 | 3.68  | 1495 | 12.69 | 1503 | 11.69 |
| 1482 | 11.69 | 1498 | 1.70  |      |       |

1466/89/95/8/1500/2/3 sold for scrap to McWilliams, Shettleston;
1471/9/84 sold for scrap to T. Ward, Inverkeithing.
1482 to Bluebell Railway, 1973.

### Western Region (Corridor Brake Seconds)

|      | Wdn.      |      | Wdn.    |      | Wdn.      |
|------|-----------|------|---------|------|-----------|
| 4210 | ?         | 4223 | c. 67   | 4318 | c. 68     |
| 4211 | ?         | 4224 | c. 67   | 4319 | c. 67     |
| 4213 | ?         | 4225 | c. 67   | 4320 | c. 11.66  |
| 4214 | c. 67     | 4226 | c. 67   | 4327 | 2.65      |
| 4215 | ?         | 4227 | c. 2.66 | 4328 | 2.65      |
| 4216 | c. 11.66  | 4228 | ?       | 4329 | c. 67     |
| 4217 | 7.68      | 4282 | c. 67   | 4330 | c. 67     |
| 4218 | 12.67     | 4307 | 2.65    | 4331 | 11.66     |
| 4219 | c. 68     | 4308 | 2.65    | 4332 | ?         |
| 4220 | 10.65     | 4309 | 2.65    | 4339 | 12.65     |
| 4221 | c. 67     | 4311 | 9.65    | 4340 | 2.65      |
| 4222 | c. 67     | 4312 | 9.65    | 4354 | c. 8.67   |
|      |           | 4317 | ?       |      |           |

4219/22-5, 4318/54 sold for scrap to Bird, Long Marston.
4329 sold to Guyana Railways early in 1967.
4211 sold to Mid-Hants Railway, March 1976.

### Western Region (Corridor Brake Composites)

|      | Wdn.  |      | Wdn.  |      | Wdn.  |
|------|-------|------|-------|------|-------|
| 6714 | 12.65 | 6717 | 11.64 | 6738 | c. 68 |
| 6715 | 2.66  | 6719 | 1.66  | 6742 | c. 67 |
| 6716 | 3.66  | 6726 | 12.64 | 6746 | c. 67 |

6742/6 sold for scrap to Bird, Long Marston. Broken up 1968.
W 6716 S was noted incorrectly painted as W 6716 W - this would have indicated a coach built
by the Great Western Railway!

## Working of Bulleid Corridor Sets, Weekdays from 26th September, 1949

†: Empty Train.
FP: Front Portion.
RP: Rear Portion.

### 2-sets (R) Nos. 63 to 75

| | | |
|---|---|---|
| am | | am |
| — | Clapham Yard | 7†51 |
| 8†00 | Waterloo | 9 0 |
| pm | | |
| 3 46 | Ilfracombe | – |
| am | | am |
| – | Clapham Yard | 10† 2 |
| 10†11 | Waterloo | 10 50 |
| pm | | pm |
| 4 32 | Ilfracombe SX | 8 30 |
| 9 09 | SX Barnstaple J. | – |
| am | | am |
| – | Clapham Yard | 10† 2 |
| 10†11 | Waterloo | 10 50 |
| pm | | |
| 4 31 | Torrington | – |
| pm | | pm |
| – | Clapham Yard SX | 12† 3 |
| | SO | 12†10 |
| 12†12 SX / 12†20 SO | Waterloo | 12 50 |
| 7 5 | Plymouth Friary | – |
| pm | Saturdays | pm |
| – | Plymouth Friary | 9 15 |
| 10 59 | Okehampton | – |
| pm | | pm |
| – | Clapham Yard | 1†58 |
| 2† 7 | Waterloo | 2 50 |
| 8 49 | Torrington | – |
| pm | SX | pm |
| – | Clapham Yard | 3†47 |
| 3†56 | Waterloo | 4 35 |
| 8 0 | Swanage | – |
| pm | FO | pm |
| – | Swanage | FP 9 28 |
| 9 52 | Wareham | – |
| am | SO | pm |
| – | Clapham Yard | 9†31 |
| 9†40 | Waterloo | 10 30 |
| pm | | |
| 1 56 | Swanage | – |
| am | | am |
| | Barnstaple J. | MX 8 0 |
| 8 46 | MX Ilfracombe | – |
| pm | | pm |
| – | Ilfracombe | 2 10 |
| 8 31 | Waterloo | 8†52 |
| † | Clapham Yard | – |
| pm | | am |
| – | Ilfracombe | 10 30 |
| 4 26 | Waterloo | 4†46 |
| † | Clapham Yard | – |
| am | | am |
| – | Plymouth Friary | 7 8 |
| 9 51 | Exeter Central | 2 30 |
| pm | | |
| 6 40 | Waterloo | 6†56 |
| † | Clapham Yard | – |
| pm | | am |
| – | Torrington | 8 10 |
| | | pm |
| 2 27 | Waterloo | 2†45 |
| † | Clapham Yard | – |
| pm | | am |
| – | Torrington | 10 30 |
| | | pm |
| 4 26 | Waterloo | 4†46 |
| † | Clapham Yard | – |
| am | | am |
| – | Wareham | SO 8 18 |
| 8 40 | SO Swanage | 9 24 |
| pm | | pm |
| 12 59 | Waterloo | 1†18 |
| † | Clapham Yard | – |

### 3-sets (L) Nos. 770 to 793, 805 to 829

| | | |
|---|---|---|
| am | MO | am |
| – | Waterloo | 2 50 |
| 6 38 | Bournemouth W. | – |
| am | Weekdays | am |
| – | Bournemouth W. | 10 12 |
| pm | | pm |
| 12 59 | Waterloo | 1†18 |
| † | Clapham Yard | – |
| am | | am |
| – | Clapham Yard | 4† 5 |
| 4†14 | Waterloo | 5 40 |
| | | pm |
| 10 07 | Weymouth | 1 25 |
| pm | | |
| 4 58 | Waterloo | 5†10 |
| † | Clapham Yard | – |
| am | MO | am |
| – | Clapham Yard | 4† 5 |
| 4†14 | Waterloo | 5 40 |
| 8 53 | Bournemouth C. | 10†10 |
| 10†19 | Bournemouth W. | – |
| am | | am |
| – | Clapham Yard | 6†43 |
| 6†52 | Waterloo | 7 20 |
| | | pm |
| 9 58 | Salisbury | 3 5 |
| pm | | |
| 6 05 | Exeter Central | 7 58 |
| 10 28 | Plymouth Friary | – |
| am | MO | am |
| – | Clapham Yard | 6†43 |
| 6†52 | Waterloo | 7 20 |
| 9 58 | Salisbury | – |
| am | | am |
| – | Clapham Yard | 7†30 |
| 7†39 | Waterloo | 8 30 |
| pm | | pm |
| 12 22 | Weymouth | 3 50 |
| 8 26 | Waterloo | 8†40 |
| † | Clapham Yard | – |
| am | | am |
| – | Clapham Yard | 7†51 |
| 8† 0 | Waterloo | 9 0 |
| pm | | pm |
| 3 36 | Plymouth Friary | 7 10 |
| 9 48 | Exeter Central | 10 0 |
| 10 37 | Honiton | 11 0 |
| 11 31 | Exeter Central | – |

### Set No. 788 (Plum and Spilt Milk)

| | | |
|---|---|---|
| am | | am |
| – | Clapham Yard | 8†02 |
| 8†11 | Waterloo | FP 9 30 |
| pm | | pm |
| 12 43 | Bournemouth W. | 3 5 |
| 6 36 | Waterloo | FP 6†47 |
| † | Clapham Yard | – |
| am | | am |
| – | Clapham Yard | 9†31 |
| 9†40 | Waterloo | 10 30 |
| pm | | pm |
| 1 47 | Weymouth | 5 35 |
| 8 58 | Waterloo | 9†20 |
| † | Clapham Yard | – |
| am | | am |
| – | Clapham Yard | 10† 2 |
| 10†11 | Waterloo | 10 50 |
| pm | | pm |
| 4 53 | Plymouth Friary | – |
| pm | SX | pm |
| – | Plymouth Friary | 9 15 |
| 10 13 | Tavistock | – |
| pm | SO | pm |
| – | Plymouth Friary | 6 16 |
| 7 17 | Tavistock | – |
| am | | am |
| – | Clapham Yard | 10†48 |
| 10†57 | Waterloo | 11 30 |
| pm | SX | pm |
| 2 22 | Bournemouth Ctl | 2 57 |
| 4 18 | Weymouth | 6 30 |
| 11 1 | Waterloo | 11†13 |
| † | Clapham Yard | – |
| pm | SO | pm |
| 2 34 | Bournemouth W. | – |
| am | Saturdays | am |
| – | Clapham Yard | 11†45 |
| | | pm |
| 11†54 | Waterloo | 12 35 |
| pm | | |
| 3 14 | Bournemouth W. | 8†15 |
| 8†24 | Bournemouth C. | 9 18 |
| 10 42 | Weymouth | – |

## 3-sets (L) - continued
## Weekdays, from 26th September, 1949

| | | |
|---|---|---|
| **pm** | | **pm** |
| – | Clapham Yard | 12†45 |
| 12 54 | Waterloo | 1 30 |
| 5 33 | Weymouth | 9 55 |
| **mdt** | | |
| 12 37 | Southampton T. | – |
| | (Forms 1.10 am to Waterloo) | |
| **pm** | | **pm** |
| – | Clapham Yard | 1†58 |
| 2† 7 | Waterloo | 2 50 |
| 9 4 | Plymouth Friary | – |
| **pm** | | **pm** |
| – | Clapham Yard | 2†46 |
| 2†54 | Waterloo | 3 20 |
| 6 5 | Bournemouth W. | – |
| **pm** | | **pm** |
| – | Clapham Yard | 3†47 |
| 3†56 | Waterloo | 4 35 |
| 8 4 | Weymouth | – |
| **pm** | | **pm** |
| – | Clapham Yard | 4†30 |
| 4†39 | Waterloo | 5 0 |
| 8 27 | Yeovil Jct. | 9 3 |
| 10 42 | Exeter Central | – |
| **pm** | **SX** | **pm** |
| – | Clapham Yard | 4†13 |
| 4†22 | Waterloo | 5 9 |
| 6 25 | Basingstoke | – |
| **pm** | **Saturdays** | **pm** |
| – | Clapham Yard | 4†30 |
| 4†39 | Waterloo | 5 0 |
| 7 8 | Salisbury | – |
| **pm** | **SX** | **pm** |
| – | Clapham Yard | 4†59 |
| 5† 7 | Waterloo | 5 30 |
| 8 44 | Bournemouth W. | – |
| **pm** | | **pm** |
| – | Clapham Yard | SX 5†24<br>SO 5†28 |
| 5†33 SX<br>5†37 SO | Waterloo | 6 0 |
| **mdt** | | |
| 12 12 | Plymouth Friary | |
| **pm** | | **pm** |
| – | Clapham Yard | 5†58 |
| 6† 7 | Waterloo | 6 30 |
| 9 55 | Weymouth | – |
| **pm** | | **pm** |
| – | Clapham Yard | 6†49 |
| 6†59 | Waterloo | 7 30 |
| **pm** | **SX** | |
| 11 4 | Bournemouth W. | – |
| **pm** | **SO** | |
| 10 51 | Bournemouth C. | |

| | | |
|---|---|---|
| **pm** | | **pm** |
| – | Clapham Yard | 8†59 |
| 9† 8 | Waterloo | 10 30 |
| **mdt** | | |
| 12 53 | Southampton T. | – |
| | (Forms 1.18 am to Dorchester) | |
| **pm** | | **pm** |
| – | Clapham Yard | 8†59 |
| 9† 8 | Waterloo | 10 30 |
| **mdt** | | |
| 12 53 | Southampton T. | |
| **am** | **SX** | **am** |
| – | Basingstoke | FP 6 35 |
| 8 8 | Waterloo | 8†18 |
| † | Clapham Yard | – |
| **am** | **SO** | **am** |
| – | Basingstoke | FP 10 40 |
| | | pm |
| 11 58 | Waterloo | RP 12 39 |
| **pm** | | |
| 1 55 | Basingstoke | – |
| **am** | | **am** |
| – | Bournemouth W. | 7 20 |
| 10 0 | Waterloo | 10†14 |
| † | Clapham Yard | – |
| | | **am** |
| – | Bournemouth W. | 8 35 |
| **pm** | | **pm** |
| 12 7 | Waterloo | 12†24 |
| † | Clapham Yard | – |
| **pm** | | **am** |
| – | Bournemouth W. | 11 2 |
| | | **pm** |
| 2 19 | Waterloo | 2†34 |
| † | Clapham Yard | – |
| **am** | | **am** |
| – | Exeter Central | 8 42 |
| | | **pm** |
| 11 25 | Plymouth Friary | 2 25 |
| **pm** | | |
| 8 31 | Waterloo | 8†52 |
| † | Clapham Yard | – |
| **am** | **MSX** | **am** |
| – | Exeter Central | 11 20 |
| **pm** | | |
| 2 11 | Salisbury | – |
| **am** | | **am** |
| – | Plymouth Friary | 5 56 |
| 11 52 | Salisbury | 1 8 |
| **pm** | | |
| 3 49 | Waterloo | 4† 0 |
| † | Clapham Yard | – |

| | | |
|---|---|---|
| | | **am** |
| – | Plymouth Friary | 8 15 |
| **pm** | | **pm** |
| 2 27 | Waterloo | 2†45 |
| † | Clapham Yard | – |
| **pm** | | **pm** |
| – | Plymouth Friary | 10 0 |
| 4 34 | Portsmouth & S'sea | – |
| **pm** | | **pm** |
| – | Plymouth Friary | 3 50 |
| 10 11 | Waterloo | 10†30 |
| † | Clapham Yard | – |
| **pm** | | **pm** |
| – | Portsmouth & S'sea | 12 15 |
| 6 12 | Plymouth Friary | – |
| **am** | | **am** |
| – | Salisbury | 9 33 |
| 11 8 | Waterloo | 11†20 |
| † | Clapham Yard | – |
| **am** | | **am** |
| – | Southampton T. | 1 10 |
| 3 53 | Waterloo | 4†28 |
| † | Clapham Yard | – |
| **am** | **MO** | **am** |
| – | Southampton T. | 1 18 |
| 3 36 | Weymouth | 8 25 |
| 10 0 | Bournemouth Ctl. | 10†10 |
| 10†19 | Bournemouth W. | – |
| **am** | | **am** |
| – | Southampton T. | 1 18 |
| 3 16 | Dorchester | 6 45 |
| 7 2 | Weymouth | 8 25 |
| 10 0 | Bournemouth Ctl. | 10†10 |
| 10†19 | Bournemouth W. | – |
| **am** | | **am** |
| – | Southampton T. | 6 0 |
| 8 36 | Waterloo | 8†50 |
| † | Clapham Yard | – |
| **am** | | **am** |
| – | Tavistock | 6 0 |
| 6 54 | Plymouth Friary | 11 35 |
| **pm** | | **pm** |
| 6 40 | Waterloo | 6†56 |
| † | Clapham Yard | – |
| **am** | | **am** |
| – | Weymouth | 7 38 |
| 10 54 | Waterloo | 11†16 |
| † | Clapham Yard | – |
| **pm** | | **am** |
| – | Weymouth | 11 30 |
| | | **pm** |
| 2 56 | Waterloo | 3†12 |
| † | Clapham Yard | – |

### 3-sets (M) Nos. 795 to 804
### Weekdays, from 26th September, 1949

| am | | am |
|---|---|---|
| - | Margate | 7 30 |
| 8 57 | Folkestone C. | RP 9 5 |
| 10 38 | Charing X | FP 11 15 |
| **pm** | | **pm** |
| 1 6 | Folkestone C. | 1 9 |
| 2 30 | Margate | - |
| **pm** | **Saturdays** | **pm** |
| - | Margate | 5 34 |
| 6 52 | Dover Priory | - |

| am | | am |
|---|---|---|
| - | Margate | 9 35 |
| 10 59 | Folkestone C. | 11 7 |
| **pm** | **SX** | **pm** |
| 12 30 | Charing X | FP 1 15 |
| 3 5 | Dover Priory | 3 9 |
| 4 16 | Margate | - |
| **pm** | **Saturdays** | **pm** |
| 12 30 | Charing X | FP 12 55 |
| 2 20 | Folkestone C. | 2 24 |
| 3 30 | Ramsgate | - |

| pm | | pm |
|---|---|---|
| - | Margate | 12 36 |
| 1 56 | Folkestone Jc. | FP 2 4 |
| 3 46 | Charing X | RP 4 15 |
| 5 40 | Folkestone C. | - |
| **pm** | **Saturdays** | **pm** |
| - | Folkestone C. | 5†50 |
| 5†55 | Folkestone Jc. | - |

| pm | | pm |
|---|---|---|
| - | Margate | 3.25 |
| 4 47 | Folkestone C. | RP 4 55 |
| 6 20 | Charing X | FP 7 15 |
| 8 40 | Folkestone C. | 8 43 |
| 10 0 | SX ⎱ Ramsgate | - |
| 10 4 | SO ⎰ | |

| am | **Saturdays** | am |
|---|---|---|
| - | Dover Marine | RP 9†25 |
| 9†37 | Folkestone Jc. | - |
| - | Folkestone Jc. | RP 2 4 |
| 3 47 | Charing X | FP 4 15 |
| 5 40 | Folkestone C. | 5 44 |
| 7 6 | Margate | - |

| am | **SX** | am |
|---|---|---|
| - | Ramsgate | RP 6 44 |
| 7 52 | Folkestone C. | RP 8 0 |
| 9 30 | Cannon St | FP 10†18 |
| | | **pm** |
| 10†53 | Rotherhithe Rd | 3† 0 |
| **pm** | (via Ludgate Hill) | |
| 4†36 | Cannon St | RP 5 0 |
| 6 4 | Ashford | 6 14 |
| | (via Canterbury West) | |
| 7 38 | Dover Priory | 7†39 |
| 7†44 | Dover Marine | - |
| **pm** | **FSX** | **pm** |
| - | Dover Marine | 8†40 |
| 8†45 | Dover Priory | 9 11 |
| 10 10 | Faversham | - |
| am | **Saturdays** | am |
| - | Ramsgate | RP 6 44 |
| 7 52 | Folkestone C. | RP 8 0 |
| 9 30 | Cannon St | FP 9†59 |
| | | **pm** |
| 10†15 | Rotherhithe Rd | RP 5† 5 |
| **pm** | | |
| 5†35 | Charing X | RP 6 15 |
| 8 34 | Dover Priory | 9 11 |
| 10 10 | Faversham | FP 10 57 |
| | | **mdt.** |
| 11 58 | Dover Priory | 12† 0 |
| **mdt.** | | |
| 12† 5 | Dover Marine | - |

| am | **SX** | am |
|---|---|---|
| - | Folkestone C. | FP 8 0 |
| 9 30 | Cannon St | RP 10†18 |
| | | **pm** |
| 10†53 | Rotherhithe Rd | RP 3† 0 |
| **pm** | (via Ludgate Hill) | |
| 4†36 | Cannon St | FP 5 0 |
| 6 4 | Ashford | 6 9 |
| 7 36 | Ramsgate | - |

| am | **Saturdays** | am |
|---|---|---|
| - | Folkestone C. | FP 8 0 |
| 9 30 | Cannon St | RP 9†59 |
| | | **pm** |
| 10†15 | Rotherhithe Rd | FP 5† 5 |
| 5†35 | Charing X | FP 6 15 |
| 8 34 | Dover Priory | 8 38 |
| 9 24 | Ramsgate | - |

| am | | am |
|---|---|---|
| - | Folkestone Jc. | MO 6†40 |
| 6†43 | MO Folkestone C. | FP 9 5 |
| 10 38 | Charing X | RP 11 15 |
| **pm** | | **pm** |
| 1 6 | Folkestone C. | RP 1 14 |
| 1 17 | Folkestone Jc. FP ⎰SX | 4† 0 |
| | ⎱SO | 4†20 |
| 4† 3 | SX ⎱ Folkestone C. FP | 4 55 |
| 4†23 | SO ⎰ | |
| 6 20 | Charing X | RP 7 15 |
| 8 40 | Folkestone C. | - |

| am | **SX** | am |
|---|---|---|
| - | Dover Marine | 9†25 |
| 10†13 | Folkestone C. | FP 11 7 |
| **pm** | | **pm** |
| 12 30 | Charing X | RP 1 15 |
| 3 5 | Dover Priory | 3†20 |
| 3†25 | Dover Marine | - |
| am | **Saturdays** | am |
| - | Dover M. | FP 9†25 |
| 9†37 | Folkestone Jc. | 9†40 |
| 9†43 | Folkestone C. | FP 11 7 |
| **pm** | | **pm** |
| 12 30 | Charing X | RP 12 55 |
| 2 20 | Folkestone C. | 2†30 |
| 2†33 | Folkestone Jc. | - |

| am | **SX** | am |
|---|---|---|
| - | Faversham | MX 6 14 |
| 7 22 | MX Dover P. | MX 7†25 |
| | | **pm** |
| 7 30 | MX Dover M. | 12†25 |
| **pm** | | |
| 12†40 | Folkestone Jc. | RP 2 4 |
| 3 46 | Charing X | FP 4 15 |
| 5 40 | Folkestone C. | 5 44 |
| 7 4 | Margate | - |

**4-sets (N) Nos. 80 to 94**
**Weekdays, from 26th September, 1949**

| | | |
|---|---|---|
| am | | am |
| – | Ramsgate | 5 31 |
| 6 32 | Folkestone Jc. | FP 6 37 |
| 8 42 | Charing X | RP 9 15 |
| am | SX | |
| 10 35 | Ashford | – |
| pm | | pm |
| – | Ashford | RP 12 46 |
| 1 40 | Tonbridge | RP 3 22 |
| 4 17 | Cannon St | FP 4 38 |
| 7 18 | Folkestone Jc. | – |
| am | **Saturdays** | pm |
| 11 21 | Dover Priory | RP 6 14 |
| pm | | |
| 8 41 | Charing X | FP 9 15 |
| 11 15 | Folkestone Jc. | 11 18 |
| am | | |
| 12 20 | Ramsgate | – |

**Two 4-sets (N)**

| | | |
|---|---|---|
| am | SX | am |
| – | Ramsgate | 6†53 |
| 7†27 | Herne Bay | 8 20 |
| 9 56 | Cannon St | 10† 8 |
| | (via Ludgate Hill) | pm |
| 10†55 | Stewarts lane | 4†38 |
| pm | (via Ludgate Hill) | |
| 5†51 | Cannon St | 6 15 |
| 8 20 | Ramsgate | – |
| pm | **Saturdays** | am |
| – | Ramsgate | 11 30 |
| | | pm |
| 2 6 | Victoria | 6 6 |
| 8 42 | Ramsgate | – |

| | | |
|---|---|---|
| am | | am |
| – | Margate | 7 3 |
| 9 15 | Tonbridge | FP 9 20 |
| | SX | |
| 10 14 | Cannon St | RP 10†36 |
| | (via Ludgate Hill) | pm |
| 11†25 | Stewarts Lane | FP 4†45 |
| pm | (via Ludgate Hill) | |
| 5†56 | Cannon St | FP 6 18 |
| 7 35 | Ashford | 7 38 |
| 9 9 | Ramsgate | MP 10 38 |
| 10 56 | Margate | – |
| am | **Saturdays** | am |
| 10 15 | Cannon St | RP 10†32 |
| | | pm |
| 11† 5 | Grove Park | FP 12†16 |
| pm | | |
| 12†48 | Charing X | RP 1 15 |
| 3 24 | Dover Priory | 7 0 |
| 7 59 | Faversham | 8 50 |
| 9 52 | Dover Priory | 10 40 |
| 11 33 | Faversham | – |

| | | |
|---|---|---|
| am | SX | am |
| – | Margate | 10 10 |
| 11 38 | Ashford | RP 11 52 |
| pm | | pm |
| 1 35 | Charing X | 3 15 |
| 5 13 | Folkestone Jc. | 5 16 |
| 6 23 | Ramsgate | RP 7 52 |
| 8 6 | Margate | – |
| am | **Saturdays** | am |
| – | Margate | 10 10 |
| 11 35 | Ashford | RP 11 49 |
| pm | | pm |
| 1 24 | Charing X | FP 1†48 |
| 1†55 | Cannon St | RP 2†32 |
| 2†39 | Charing X | FP 3 15 |
| 5 18 | Folkestone Jc. | 5 20 |
| 6 44 | Margate | – |

| | | |
|---|---|---|
| am | SX | am |
| – | Ashford | 7 27 |
| 8 7 | Paddock Wood | FP 8 20 |
| 9 24 | Cannon St | RP 9 27 |
| 9 35 | Charing X | FP 9†55 |
| | | pm |
| 10†20 | Rotherhithe Rd | 2†40 |
| pm | | |
| 3† 6 | Grove Park | RP 4†10 |
| 4†32 | Charing X | FP 4†58 |
| 5†21 | Cannon St | RP 5 41 |
| 7 26 | Ashford | – |
| am | **Saturdays** | am |
| – | Ashford | FP 7 27 |
| 9 24 | Cannon St | RP 9 27 |
| 9 35 | Charing X | FP 9†55 |
| 10†15 | Rotherhithe Rd | |
| | (7.15 am Charing X to Ramsgate Sundays) | |

| | | |
|---|---|---|
| am | | am |
| – | Dover Marine | RP 9†15 |
| 9†19 | Dover Priory | 9 22 |
| | | pm |
| 11 27 | Victoria | FP 2 6 |
| pm | SX | pm |
| 3 37 | Faversham | 3 41 |
| 4 39 | Dover Priory | RP 5† 8 |
| 5†13 | Dover Marine | – |
| pm | **Saturdays** | am |
| 3 34 | Faversham | 3 38 |
| 4 38 | Dover Priory | 4†45 |
| 4†50 | Dover Marine | – |

| | | |
|---|---|---|
| am | | am |
| – | Faversham | 7 35 |
| 8 47 | Dover Priory | 8†50 |
| 8†54 | Dover M. | FP 9†15 |
| 9†19 | Dover Priory | FP 9 22 |
| | | pm |
| 11 27 | Victoria | RP 2 6 |

| | | |
|---|---|---|
| pm | SX | pm |
| 3 37 | Faversham | 3 46 |
| 4 50 | Ramsgate | RP 9 10 |
| 10 12 | Faversham | – |
| pm | **Saturdays** | pm |
| 3 34 | Faversham | 3 43 |
| 4 50 | Ramsgate | RP 6 20 |
| 6 34 | Margate | – |

| | | |
|---|---|---|
| am | | am |
| – | Folkestone Jc. | 6 37 |
| 8 42 | Charing X | FP 9 15 |
| am | SX | am |
| 10 35 | Ashford | 10 40 |
| pm | | pm |
| 12 12 | Ramsgate | 5 36 |
| 6 47 | Ashford | RP 7 8 |
| 8 41 | Charing X | 9 15 |
| 10 39 | Ashford | 10 44 |
| am | | |
| 12 20 | Ramsgate | – |
| am | **Saturdays** | am |
| 11 21 | Dover Priory | 11 26 |
| pm | | pm |
| 12 16 | Ramsgate | 5 18 |
| 6 8 | Dover Priory | FP 6 14 |
| 8 41 | Charing X | RP 9 15 |
| 11 15 | Folkestone Jc. | – |

| | | |
|---|---|---|
| am | SX | am |
| – | Folkestone Jc. | 11 16 |
| 11.44 | Ashford | FP 11 52 |
| pm | | pm |
| 1 35 | Charing X | RP 3 15 |
| 5 13 | Folkestone Jc. | – |
| am | **Saturdays** | am |
| – | Folkestone Jc. | 11 14 |
| 11 43 | Ashford | FP 11 49 |
| pm | | pm |
| 1 24 | Charing X | RP 1†48 |
| 1†55 | Cannon St | FP 2†32 |
| 2†39 | Charing X | 3 15 |
| 5 18 | Folkestone Jc. | – |

| | | |
|---|---|---|
| am | | am |
| – | Stewarts Lane | RP 7†40 |
| 7†50 | Victoria | FP 8 35 |
| 9 30 | Chatham | 9 33 |
| | | pm |
| 11 0 | Ramsgate | 1 10 |
| pm | | |
| 2 13 | Faversham | FP 2 19 |
| 3 48 | Victoria | RP 4† 0 |
| 4†10 | Stewarts Lane | – |

## 4-sets (N) - continued
## Weekdays, from 26th September, 1949

| am | | am |
|---|---|---|
| -- | Stewarts Lane | FP 7+40 |
| 7+50 | Victoria | RP 8 35 |
| 9 30 | Chatham | 9 38 |
| 11 13 | Dover Priory | 11+16 |
| | | **pm** |
| 11+21 | Dover Marine {SX | 1+ 0 |
| **pm** | {SO | 12+55 |
| 1+ 4 SX } | Dover Pr. {SX | 1 10 |
| 1+ 0 SO } | {SO | 1  8 |
| 2 10 | Faversham | RP 2 19 |
| 3 48 | Victoria | FP 4+ 0 |
| 4+10 | Stewarts Lane | -- |

**5 Buffet 'set', formed:**
1 cor. bke. compo (new)
1 cor. third (1932/6 series)
1 refreshment saloon
1 kitchen buffet car
1 cor. bke. compo (new)

| am | | am |
|---|---|---|
| -- | Exeter Central | 7 30 |
| 11 8 | Waterloo | 11+20 |
| **pm** | | |
| + | Clapham Yard {SX | 5+24 |
| | {SO | 5+28 |
| 5+33 SX } | Waterloo | 6  0 |
| 5+37 SO } | | |
| 10 6 | Exeter Central | -- |

**4-set 'N' plus 2 Pullmans**
(3 Pullmans until 29 Oct.)
'Thanet Belle'

| am | SX | am |
|---|---|---|
| -- | Stewarts Lane | 10+55 |
| 11+ 5 | Victoria | 11 35 |
| **pm** | | **pm** |
| 2 19 | Ramsgate | 5  5 |
| 7  5 | Victoria | 7+25 |
| 7+35 | Stewarts Lane | -- |
| **am** | **Saturdays** | **am** |
| -- | Stewarts Lane | 10+45 |
| 10+55 | Victoria | 11 35 |
| **pm** | | **pm** |
| 1 58 | Ramsgate | 5  5 |
| 7 10 | Victoria | 7+26 |
| 7+36 | Stewarts Lane | -- |

**6 Dining Set No. 299**
**(Plum & Spilt Milk)**

| am | | am |
|---|---|---|
| -- | Clapham Yard | FP 8+ 2 |
| 8+11 | Waterloo | RP 9 30 |
| **pm** | | **pm** |
| 12 43 | B'mouth West | 2 20 |
| 2 28 | B'mouth Ctl | RP 2 40 |
| 4 58 | Waterloo | FP 5+10 |
| + | Clapham Yard | -- |

| am | SX | am |
|---|---|---|
| -- | Tonbridge | RP 9 20 |
| 10 14 | Cannon St | FP 10+36 |
| | (via Ludgate Hill) | **pm** |
| 11+25 | Stewarts Lane | RP 4+45 |
| **pm** | (via Ludgate Hill) | |
| 5+56 | Cannon St | RP 6 18 |
| 7 35 | Ashford | 9 20 |
| 10 11 | Tonbridge | -- |
| **am** | **Saturdays** | **am** |
| -- | Tonbridge | RP 9 20 |
| 10 15 | Cannon St | FP 10+32 |
| | | **pm** |
| 11+ 5 | Grove Park | RP 12+16 |
| 12+48 | Charing X | FP 1 15 |
| 3 24 | Dover Priory | 3 28 |
| 4 33 | Margate | 6 58 |
| 8 32 | Ashford | 9 20 |
| 10 11 | Tonbridge | -- |

## Working of Miscellaneous Sets, Weekdays, from 14th June, 1954

**10 Buffet Set 266**

| am | | am |
|---|---|---|
| -- | Ramsgate | 6 29 |
| 8 54 | Cannon St | 9+ 3 |
| **am** | **SX** | **am** |
| 9+20 | Blackheath | 10+34 |
| | | **pm** |
| 11+ 5 | Stewarts Lane | 4+15 |
| **pm** | (via Ludgate Hill) | |
| 5+28 | Cannon St | 5 45 |
| 8  2 | Ramsgate | -- |
| **am** | **Saturdays** | **am** |
| 8 54 | Cannon St | 9+ 3 |
| | (via Ludgate Hill) | |
| 9+50 | Stewarts Lane | 11+10 |
| **pm** | (via Ludgate Hill) | **pm** |
| 12+12 | Cannon St | 12 45 |
| 2 53 | Ramsgate | -- |

**10 Buffet Set 267**

| am | | am |
|---|---|---|
| -- | Ramsgate | 7 20 |
| 9 19 | Cannon St | 9+30 |
| | (via Ludgate Hill) | |
| **am** | **SX** | **am** |
| 10+35 | Stewarts Lane | 3+30 |
| **pm** | (via Ludgate Hill) | |
| 4+47 | Cannon St | 5 15 |
| 7 12 | Ramsgate | -- |
| **am** | **Saturdays** | **am** |
| 10+35 | Stewarts Lane | 11+50 |
| **pm** | (via Ludgate Hill) | **pm** |
| 12+48 | Cannon St | 1 15 |
| 3 29 | Ramsgate | -- |

**8 Buffet Set 265**
**Plus 1 Cor. Compo**

| am | SX | am |
|---|---|---|
| -- | Ramsgate | 7 35 |
| 9 36 | Cannon St | 9+43 |
| | | **pm** |
| 10+ 2 | Rotherhithe Rd | 3+ 8 |
| **pm** | | |
| 3+33 | Cannon St | 4 45 |
| 6 55 | Ramsgate | -- |

**1 Cor. Third on 7.35 am**
**Up Mondays and 4.45 pm**
**Down Fridays. Rotherhithe**
**Road to provide.**
**Saturdays**
(Plus 2 Cor. Thirds)

| pm | | pm |
|---|---|---|
| -- | Ramsgate | 12 20 |
| 2 50 | Victoria | 3 20 |
| 5 24 | Ramsgate | -- |

## Working of Miscellaneous Sets - continued
### Weekdays, from 14th June, 1954

| | 6 Cor. Set 264 Plus 2 Cor. Thirds | |
|---|---|---|
| am | SX | am |
| -- | Ramsgate | 6†53 |
| 7†27 | Herne Bay | 8 20 |
| 9 56 | Cannon St | 10† 8 |
| | (via Ludgate Hill) | pm |
| 10†55 | Stewarts Lane | 4†35 |
| pm | (via Ludgate Hill) | |
| 5†48 | Cannon St | 6 16 |
| 8 22 | Ramsgate | -- |
| | **Saturdays** | |
| am | **Plus 3 Cor. Thirds** | am |
| -- | Ramsgate | 9 25 |
| 11 49 | Victoria | 11†57 |
| pm | | pm |
| † | Sidings | 3†23 |
| 3†28 | Victoria | 4 6 |
| 6 46 | Ramsgate | -- |

| | 1 Cor. Third, SX, 8 Cor. Set 474, 2 Cor. Thirds | |
|---|---|---|
| am | | am |
| -- | Ramsgate | 6 6 |
| 8 28 | Cannon St | 8†34 |
| | (via Ludgate Hill) | |
| am | SX | am |
| 9†28 | Victoria | 9†40 |
| † | Sidings | 9†49 |
| 9†54 | Victoria | 10 35 |
| pm | | pm |
| 1 10 | Ramsgate | -- |
| pm | **Set 474 only.** | pm |
| -- | Ramsgate | 4 15 |
| 7 22 | Victoria | 7†38 |
| † | Sidings | 7†50 |
| 7†55 | Victoria | 8 35 |
| 11 12 | Ramsgate | -- |
| am | **Saturdays** | am |
| 9†26 | Victoria | 9 50 |
| pm | | pm |
| 12 17 | Ramsgate | 12†35 |
| 1† 5 | Deal | 2 20 |
| 4 50 | Charing Cross | 5 15 |
| 7 28 | Deal | 7†32 |
| 7†40 | Sandwich | -- |
| | (9†10 pm to Ramsgate Sundays) | |

| | 7 Buffet Set 473, Plus 1 Cor. Third, SX 2 Cor. Thirds, SO | |
|---|---|---|
| am | SX | am |
| -- | Ramsgate | 8 25 |
| 10 27 | Victoria | 10†40 |
| † | Sidings | 11†55 |
| noon | | pm |
| 12† 0 | Victoria | 12 35 |
| pm | | |
| 3 22 | Ramsgate | -- |
| am | **Saturdays** | am |
| -- | Ramsgate | 8 20 |
| 10 28 | Victoria | 11 35 |
| pm | | pm |
| 1 52 | Ramsgate | 3 30 |
| 5 54 | Victoria | 6† 8 |
| 6†18 | Stewarts Lane | 8†50 |
| 9† 0 | Victoria | 9 35 |
| mdt. | | |
| 12 0 | Ramsgate | -- |

| | 9 Buffet Set 875, 1 Cor. Third | |
|---|---|---|
| am | SX | am |
| -- | Ramsgate | 9 25 |
| 11 46 | Victoria | 12† 0 |
| pm | | pm |
| † | Sidings | 2†55 |
| 3† 0 | Victoria | 3 35 |
| 6 8 | Ramsgate | -- |
| pm | **Saturdays** | am |
| -- | Ramsgate | 10 10 |
| | | pm |
| 12 22 | Victoria | 1 20 |
| 3 37 | Ramsgate | 5 10 |
| 7 10 | Victoria | 7†25 |
| † | Sidings | 8†13 |
| 8†18 | Victoria | 8 35 |
| 11 12 | Ramsgate | -- |

| | 9 Buffet Set 874 | |
|---|---|---|
| pm | SX | pm |
| -- | Ramsgate | 3 22 |
| 6 12 | Victoria | 7 35 |
| 10 1 | Ramsgate | -- |
| pm | **Saturdays** | pm |
| - | Ramsgate | 9 46 |
| | | pm |
| 12 11 | Victoria | 12 55 |
| 3 14 | Ramsgate | 7 45 |
| 10 20 | Victoria | 10†40 |
| 10†50 | Stewarts Lane | -- |
| | (9.40 am Victoria - Ramsgate Sundays) | |

| | 9 Cor. Set 263 T.W.Th.O., 13 July to 26 August, 1954 | |
|---|---|---|
| am | | am |
| -- | Stewarts Lane | 7†55 |
| 8† 5 | Victoria | 8 30 |
| 10 41 | Ramsgate | 11†35 |
| | | pm |
| 11†50 | Margate | 7 35 |
| pm | | |
| 9 46 | Victoria | 10† 8 |
| 10†18 | Stewarts Lane | -- |
| am | **Saturdays** | am |
| -- | Stewarts Lane | 8†35 |
| 8†48 | Victoria | 9 8 |
| | | pm |
| 11 47 | Ramsgate | 1† 0 |
| pm | | |
| 1†34 | Herne Bay | 2 24 |
| 4 11 | Victoria | 4†27 |
| † | Sidings | -- |

### Working of 6-Dining Sets Nos. 290 to 300
### 15th September, 1952, until further notice

**Weekdays**

| Wkg. No. | Set No. | | |
|---|---|---|---|
| 37 | 296 | 8.30 am | Waterloo to Bournemouth West and 1.5 pm return. |
| 38 | 299 | 9.30 am | Waterloo to Bournemouth West and 2.20 pm return. |
| 39 | 295 | 10.30 am | Waterloo to Bournemouth West and 3.5 pm return. |
| 40 | 300 | 11.30 am | Waterloo to Bournemouth West and 5.5 pm return. |
| 41 | 292 | 1.30 pm | Waterloo to Bournemouth West and 6.16 pm return. |
| 42 | 297 | 7.20 am | Bournemouth West to Waterloo and 3.20 pm return. |
| 43 | 293 | 8.35 am | Bournemouth West to Waterloo and 3.30 pm return. |
| 44 | 291 | | Spare set. |
| 45 | 294 | 11. 5 am | Bournemouth West to Waterloo and 5.30 return. |
| 46 | 290 | 12.20 pm | Bournemouth West to Waterloo and 7.30 pm return. |
| 47 | 298 | | Spare set. |

### Working of Kitchen Buffet Cars (Tavern Type) and Saloons
### 15th September, 1952, until further notice

| Wkg. No. | Car | Saloon | |
|---|---|---|---|
| 1 | 7896 | 7835 | 9.0 am Waterloo to Exeter Ctl. and 2.30 pm return. |
| 2 | 7895 | 7839 | 11.0 am Waterloo to Exeter Ctl and 4.30 pm return. |
| 3 | 7894 | 7833 | 1.0 pm Waterloo to Exeter Ctl and 5.55 pm return. |
| 4 | 7892 | 7838 | Spare car. |
| 5 | 7893 | 7836 | 7.30 am Exeter Ctl to Waterloo and 3.0 pm return. |
| 6 | 7899 | 7837 | (Alternate days) 5.0 pm Waterloo to Yeovil Jc., thence 9.0 pm to Exeter Central. (Alternate days) 12.31 pm Exeter Central to Waterloo. |
| 7 | 7897 | 7834 | 10.30 am Exeter Central to Waterloo and 6.o pm return. |
| 8 | 7898 | 7840 | 8.20 am Bournemouth West to Waterloo and 4.35 pm return ('Royal Wessex') |

### Working of Bulleid Sets on the Oxted Line, Mondays to Fridays
### from 13th June, 1955, until further notice.

**3-sets (L) Nos. 768, 769 and 850**

| am | | am |
|---|---|---|
| -- | Tun. W. W. | FP 5†40 |
| 6† 3 | Forest Row | 6 22 |
| 6 50 | Three Bridges | 7  7 |
| 7 33 | Forest Row | FP 8 24 |
| 9 36½ | Victoria | RP 9†50 |
| | | pm |
| 10† 7 | Eardley | FP 4†39 |
| **pm** | | |
| 4†55 | Victoria | RP 5  9 |
| 7  1 | Tunbridge W. W. | 7 47 |
| 9 32 | Victoria | 10  8 |
| **mdt.** | | |
| 12  0 | Tunbridge W. W. | -- |

| am | | am |
|---|---|---|
| -- | Tun. W.W.**MX** | RP 5†40 |
| 6† 3 | MX Forest Row | -- |
| -- | Forest Row | RP 8 24 |
| 9 36½ | Victoria | FP 9†50 |
| | | pm |
| 10† 7 | Eardley | RP 4†39 |
| **pm** | | |
| 4†55 | Victoria | FP 5  9 |
| 7  1 | Tunbridge W. W. | 9 15 |
| 10 41 | Victoria | 11† 0 |
| † | Sidings | -- |

| am | | am |
|---|---|---|
| -- | Vic. Sth. Sdgs. | 5†30 |
| 5†31 | Victoria | 6 29 |
| 8 46 | Tunbridge W. W. | 9  8 |
| | | pm |
| 10 29 | Eastbourne | 1  9 |
| **pm** | | |
| 1 28 | Hailsham | 2  0 |
| 2 16 | Eastbourne | 3 43 § |
| 5  9 | Tunbridge W. W. | 5 38 |
| 6 40 | Brighton | FP 6 52 |
| 8  1 | Tunbridge W. W. | -- |
| | § Plus 1 Cor. Third | |

**3-sets (M) Nos. 795-801**
**Plus 1 Cor. 1st**

| am | | am |
|---|---|---|
| -- | Brighton | 8 20 |
| 9 17 | Eridge | FP 9 23½ |
| 10 21 | Victoria | RP 10†28 |
| **pm** | | **pm** |
| † | Sidings | RP 3†30 |
| 3†32 | Victoria | FP 3 52 |
| 4 51 | Eridge | 4 54 |
| 5 53 | Brighton | -- |

**Plus 1 Cor. 3rd**

| pm | | pm |
|---|---|---|
| -- | E. Grinstead FP | 4  9 |
| 5 20 | London Bdg. RP | 5 40 |
| 6 46 | E. G'stead | FO 6†54 |
| 7† 1 | FO Forest Row | -- |
| **am** | | **am** |
| -- | Tun. W. W. | FP 6 42 |
| 8  7 | Victoria | RP 8†13 |
| † | Sidings | MP 10†36 |
| 10†38 | Victoria | MP 11  8 |
| 11 25 | E. Croydon | RP 11 29 |
| **pm** | | **pm** |
| 12 14 | Eridge | 12 24 |
| 1 27 | Brighton | 3  5 |
| 4 19 | Tunbridge W. W. | -- |

| am | | am |
|---|---|---|
| -- | Tun. W. W. | RP 6 42 § |
| 8  7 | Victoria | FP 8†13 § |
| † | Sidings | RP 10†36 |
| 10†38 | Victoria | FP 11  8 |
| 11 25 | E. Croydon | FP 11 29 |
| **pm** | | **pm** |
| 12 14 | Eridge | 12 18 |
| 1 35 | Eastbourne | 5 56 |
| 7 24 | Tunbridge W. W. | -- |
| | § Plus 1 Cor. Third | |

## Working of Bulleid Sets on the Oxted Line
### Mondays to Fridays - continued

| am | | am |
|---|---|---|
| -- | Victoria MO RP | 6 29 |
| 8 46 | MO Tun. W. W. | 9 47 |
| | | **pm** |
| 11 28 | Victoria | 12 8 |
| **pm** | | |
| 2 0 | Tunbridge W. W. | 2 47 |
| 4 35 | Victoria | 4†40 |
| † | Sidings    RP | 5†52 * |
| 5†54 | Victoria    FP | 6 10 * |
| 6 28 | East Croydon | 6 30 * |
| 7 33 | Uckfield | -- |

\* Plus 1 Cor. 1st, 2 Cor. 3rds.

| am | | am |
|---|---|---|
| -- | Uckfield | 8 23 * |
| 9 47 | Victoria | 10 8 |
| **noon** | | **pm** |
| 12 0 | Tunbridge W. W. | 12 47 |
| **pm** | | |
| 2 39 | Victoria | 3 8 |
| 4 24 | E. Grinstead | 7 23 |
| 8 32 | Victoria | 9 8 |
| 11 0 | Tunbridge W. W. | -- |

\* Plus 1 Cor. 1st, 2 Cor. 3rds.

### 8 Set 767

| am | | am |
|---|---|---|
| - | Tunbridge W. W. | 7 49 |
| 9 14 | London Bridge | 9 21 |
| 9†28 | New Cross Gate | 10†53 |
| | | **pm** |
| 11†21 | Eardley | 5†19 |
| **pm** | | |
| 5†36 | Victoria | 5 50 |
| 7 37 | Tunbridge W. W. | -- |

### 5 Set 802, / 2 Cor. Thirds

| am | | am |
|---|---|---|
| - | Forest Row | 7 4 |
| 8 19 | London Bridge | 8†33 |
| | | **pm** |
| 8†40 | New Cross Gate | 6† 7 |
| **pm** | | |
| 6†14 | London Bridge | 6 30 |
| 7 50 | Forest Row | -- |

### 6 Set 876

| am | | am |
|---|---|---|
| - | Brighton | 7 6 |
| 9 28 | London Bridge | 9†37 |
| | | **pm** |
| 9†45 | New Cross Gate | 4† 8 |
| **pm** | | |
| 4†15 | London Bridge | 4 40 |
| 6 15 | Uckfield | 6†40 |
| 7† 7 | Tunbridge W. W. | 7 39 |
| 8 50 | Brighton | -- |

## Working of Bulleid Sets on the Oxted Line
### Mondays to Fridays, from 13th June, 1960

### 4 Set 'N'

| am | | am |
|---|---|---|
| - | E. Grinstead    FP | 7 41 |
| 8 45 | London Bdg.    RP | 8†53 |
| | | **pm** |
| 9† 0 | New Cross Gt    FP | 3†33 |
| **pm** | | |
| 3†40 | London Bdg.    RP | 4 20 |
| 4 36 | East Croydon | 4 44 |
| 5 51 | Tunbridge W.W. | 9 20 |
| 10 45 | Victoria | 11 38 |
| **mdt** | | |
| 12 56½ | E. Grinstead | -- |

### 8 Set 767

| am | | am |
|---|---|---|
| - | Groombridge | 7 55½ |
| 9 13 | London Bridge | 9†21 |
| 9†28 | New Cross Gate | 10†53 |
| | | **pm** |
| 11†21 | Eardley | 5†19 |
| **pm** | | |
| 5†36 | Victoria | 5 49 |
| 7 33 | Groombridge | -- |

### 5 Set 801 or 802 / 2 2nds (100 seats)

| am | | am |
|---|---|---|
| -' | Tunbridge W. W. | 8 26 |
| 10 6½ | London Bdg. | 10†30 |
| | | **pm** |
| 10†37 | New Cross Gate | 6† 7 |
| **pm** | | |
| 6† 14 | London Bridge | 6 31 |
| 7 50 | Forest Row | |

### 4 Set 'N'

| am | | am |
|---|---|---|
| - | E. Grinstead | 6 34≠ |
| 7 43 | London Bridge | 8 1≠ |
| | | **pm** |
| 9 59 | Tun. W. W.    RP | 1 47 |
| 3 12 | E. Croydon | 3 44 |
| 4 38 | E. Grinstead | 5 26* |
| 6 38 | Victoria | 6 48* |
| 8 | 3½ E. Grinstead | -- |

≠ Plus 2 2nds (100 seats)
\* Plus 1 2nd (100 seats)

### 5 Set 801 or 802

| am | | am |
|---|---|---|
| - | Forest Row | 7 0* |
| 8 16 | London Bridge | 8†33* |
| | | **pm** |
| 8†40 | New Cross Gate | 3†18≠ |
| **pm** | | |
| 3†25 | London Bridge | 5 37≠ |
| 6 45 | E. Grinstead | 7 26§ |
| 8 33 | Victoria | 9 8§ |
| 10 59 | Tunbridge W. W. | -- |

\* Plus 2 2nds (100 seats)
≠ Plus 1 Cor. Compo, / 2 2nds (100 seats)
§ Plus 1 Cor. Compo.

### 5 Set 803 or 804

| am | | am |
|---|---|---|
| - | E. Grinstead    RP | 7 41 |
| 8 45 | London Br.    FP | 8†53 |
| | | **pm** |
| 9† 0 | New Cross G.    RP | 3†33 |
| **pm** | | |
| 3†40 | London Bridge FP | 4 20 |
| 4 36 | East Croydon | 4 38 |
| 5 20 | East Grinstead | -- |

### 6 Set 876

| am | | am |
|---|---|---|
| - | Brighton | 7 17 |
| 9 28 | london Bridge | 9†37 |
| | | **pm** |
| 9†45 | New Cross Gate | 3†48 |
| **pm** | | |
| 3†55 | London Bridge | 4 40 |
| 6 52 | Brighton | -- |

### 6 Set 897

| am | | am |
|---|---|---|
| -- | Tun. W. W.    FP | 7 12 |
| 8 41½ | Victoria    RP | 9 9 |
| | | **pm** |
| 10 59 | Tunbridge W. W. | ·3 47 |
| **pm** | | |
| 5 11 | East Croydon | 5†27 |
| 5†46 | London Bridge | 6 15 |
| 7 36 | Tunbridge W. W. | |

1. Standard type SR torpedo vent
2. Combined door top light and vent
3. End step & bracket fixed to underframe
4. Lower step and hanger bracket on U frame
5. Guard's lookout periscope
6. Standard SR 10in high sliding window vent
6A. as above but BR standard 15in high
7. Mushroom type lavatory vent
8. Lavatory window with 10in sliding vent
8A. as above but BR type
9. Water tank top and filler
10. Brackets for roof destination boards
11. Passenger emergency brake application cock and operating gear
12. Water tank filler nozzles
13. 3rd class compartment seating (dotted)
14. 3rd class saloon type seating (dotted)
15. 1st class compartment seating (dotted)
16. Handrail for step ends
17. Handbrake column and wheel for guard
18. Reservation board (small)
19. Destination board (small)
20. Roof destination board
21. Corridor handrails (inside window)
22. Handrail and tank filler pipe
23. 1st class compartment seating
24. 1st class dining saloon chairs (dotted)
25. 1st class dining saloon tables and lamps
26. Dining saloon curtains
27. 3rd class dining saloon chairs (dotted)
28. 3rd class dining saloon tables and lamps
29. Extract propellor fans
30. Kitchen cooking range ventilator
31. Lighting control jumper cables
32. Lamp irons or brackets
33. Lamp iron secured to footstep
34. Handrail
35. Coach end footstep
36. Builders weight and dimension plates
37. Long stepboard across two of item 35
38. Set number
39. Pullman type vestibule connection
40. Filler pipe support bracket
41. Expanded metal screen for luggage
42. Door hinge
43. Door steps
44. Door handles
45. Commode handles
46. Rainstrip on roof
47. Cant strip
48. Monsoon ventilators

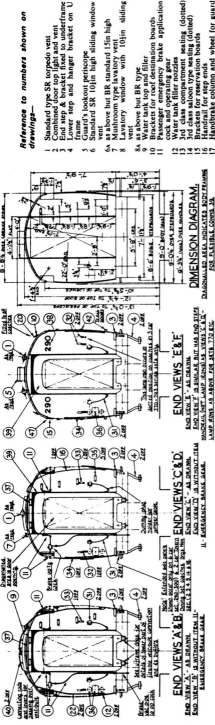

DIMENSION DIAGRAM.

DIAGONALLED AREA INDICATES BODY FRAMING FOR FLEXIBLE CONNS 39.

END VIEWS 'E' & 'F'.

END VIEW 'E' - AS DRAWN.
END VIEW 'F' IS SIMILAR BUT HAS END STEPS HANDRAIL (NOT LAMP IRONS) AS VIEWS 'C' & 'D'. LAMP IRONS AS ABOVE FOR SKTS 772 KIC.

END VIEWS 'C' & 'D'.

END VIEW 'C' - AS DRAWN.
END VIEW 'D' IS WITHOUT ITEM 11 - EMERGENCY BRAKE GEAR.

END VIEWS 'A' & 'B'.

END VIEW 'A' - AS DRAWN.
END VIEW 'B' IS WITHOUT ITEM 11 - EMERGENCY BRAKE GEAR.

NOTE:— ALL COACH END FITTINGS SHOULD BE TAKEN FROM DETAILS GIVEN ON THIS DRG. RATHER THAN FROM THE BODY DRGS. WHERE END DETAILS ARE SHOWN.

THESE END VIEWS & DETAILS APPLY TO ALL SOUTHERN RY. MAIN LINE STOCK BUILT 1945-1951.

PERISCOPE. FITTED TO BRAKE END COACHES.

LONGER WATER TANK AS FITTED TO CERTAIN SALOON COACHES.

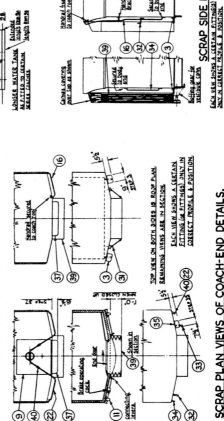

SCRAP SIDE ELEVATION OF COACH-END DETAILS.

EACH VIEW SHOWS A CERTAIN FITTING(S) ONLY IN CORRECT PROFILE & POSITION.

R.H END VIEW IS A SCRAP SECTION.

TOP VIEW ON BOTH SIDES IS ROOF PLAN. REMAINING VIEWS ARE IN SECTION.

EACH VIEW SHOWS A CERTAIN FITTING (OR FITTINGS) ONLY IN CORRECT PROFILE & POSITION.

SCRAP PLAN VIEWS OF COACH-END DETAILS.

Drawings by kind permission of S.W. Stevens-Stratton Model Railway Constructor 1969.

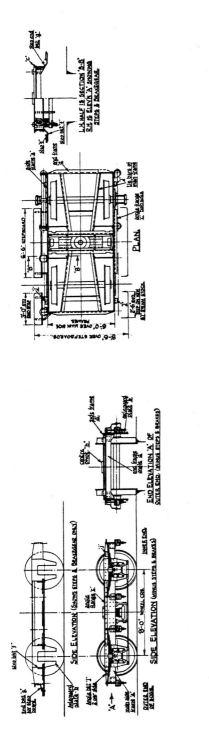

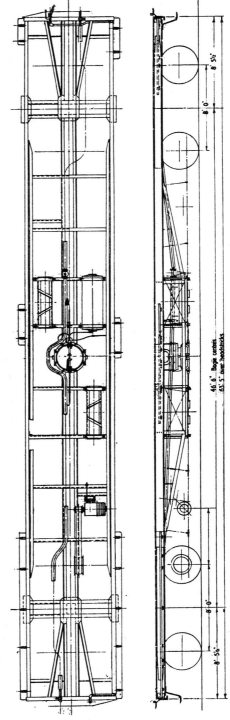

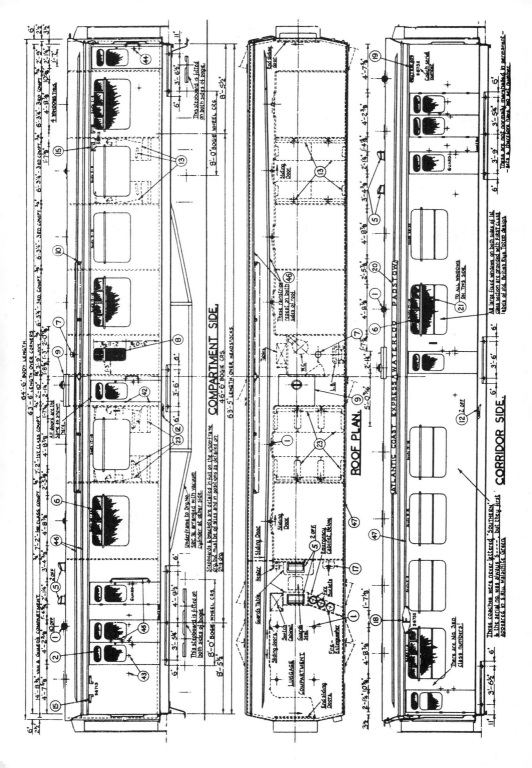

COMPARTMENT SIDE.

ROOF PLAN.

CORRIDOR SIDE.

ATLANTIC COAST EXPRESS—WATERLOO—PADSTOW.

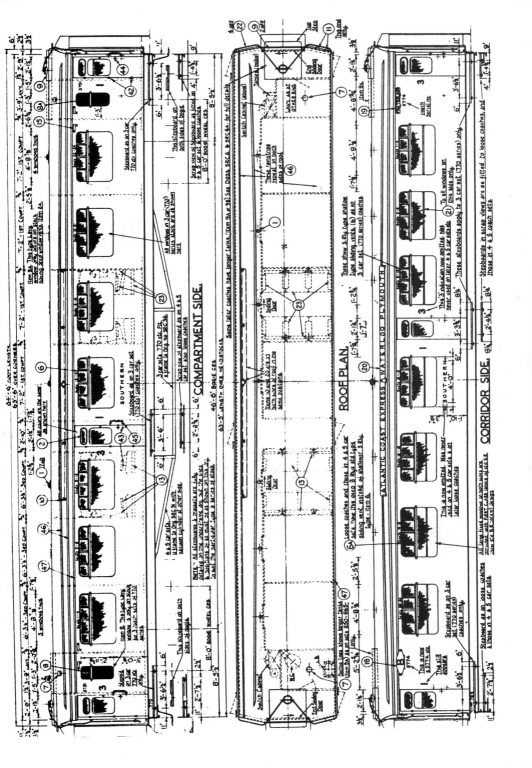

ATLANTIC COAST EXPRESS (WATERLOO—PLYMOUTH)

SOUTHERN

COMPARTMENT SIDE

ROOF PLAN

CORRIDOR SIDE

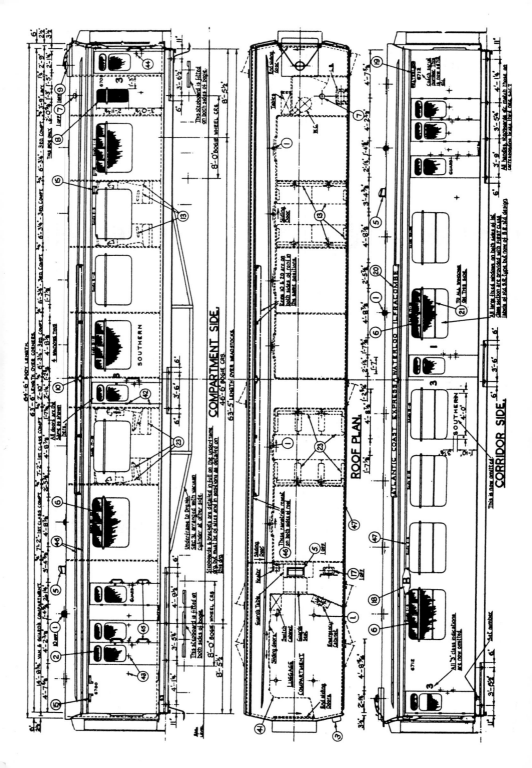

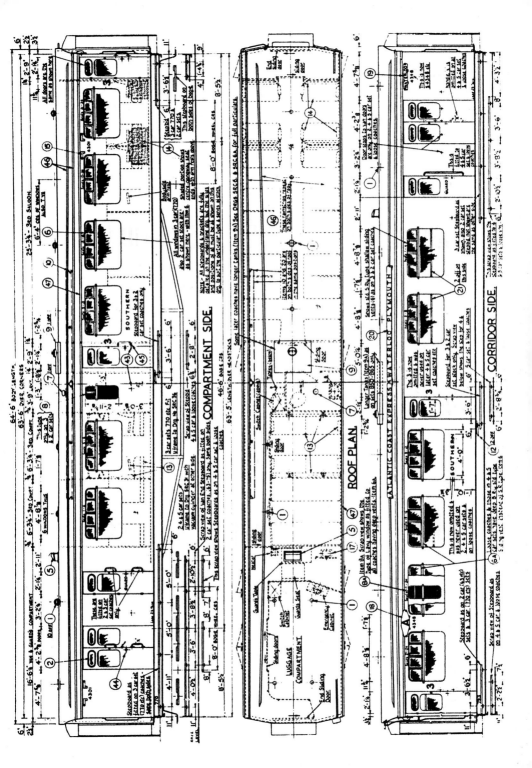

ATLANTIC COAST EXPRESS—WATERLOO ± PLYMOUTH

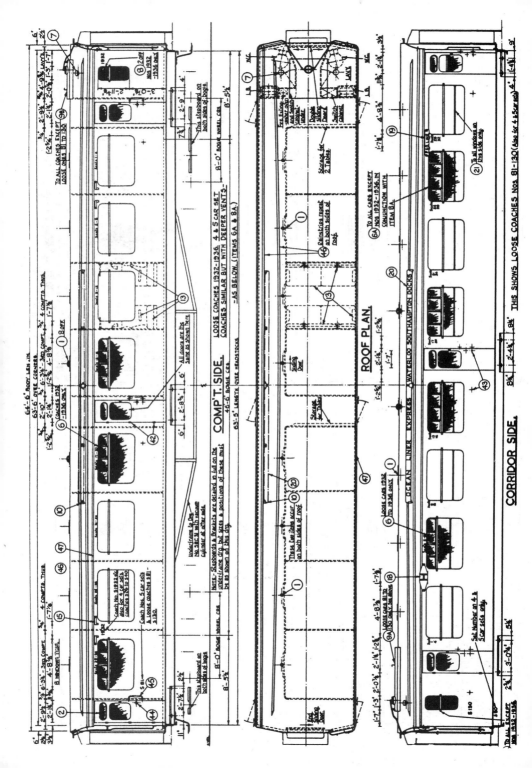

COMP'T. SIDE.

LOOSE COACHES 1932-1936. 4 & 5 CAR SET COACHES SIMILAR BUT WITH DEEPER VENTS—
—AS BELOW. (ITEMS 6A & 8A)

ROOF PLAN.

OCEAN LINER EXPRESS WATERLOO SOUTHAMPTON DOCKS.

CORRIDOR SIDE.

THIS SHOWS LOOSE COACHES Nos. B1-130 (Also for 4 & 5 car sets.)

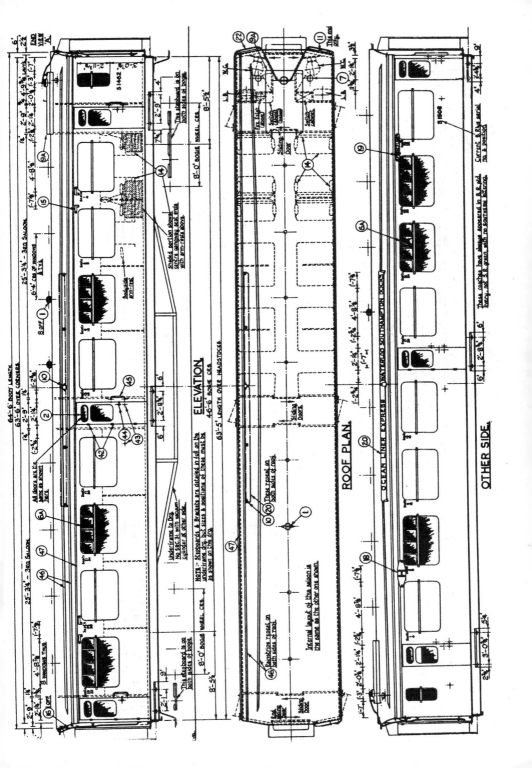

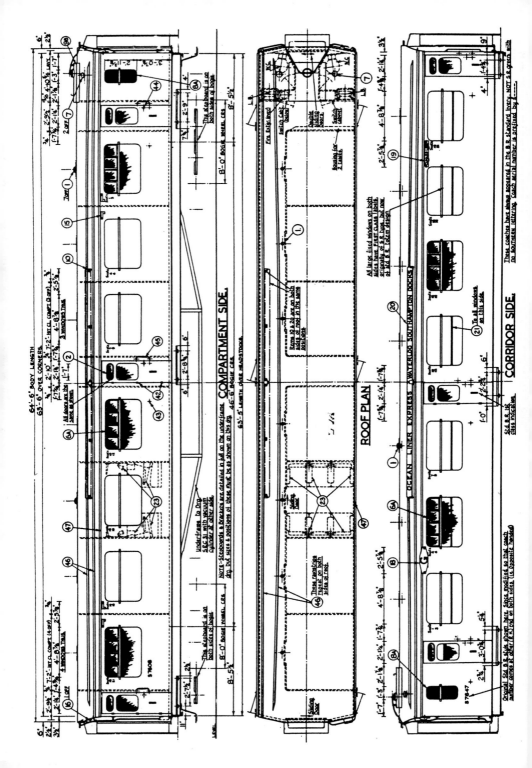